The Complete Guide to

CREDIT REPAIR

Bill Kelly, Jr.

Adams Media Corporation
Avon, Massachusetts

Copyright ©2001, Bill Kelly, Jr. All rights reserved. This book, or parts thereof, may not be reproduced in any form without permission from the publisher; exceptions are made for brief excerpts used in published reviews.

Published by
Adams Media Corporation
57 Littlefield Street, Avon MA 02322. U.S.A.
www.adamsmedia.com

ISBN: 1-58062-375-1

Printed in Canada.

J I H G F E D C

Library of Congress Cataloging-in-Publication Data available
upon request from the publisher

This publication is designed to provide accurate and authoritative information with regard to the subject matter covered. It is sold with the understanding that the publisher is not engaged in rendering legal, accounting, or other professional advice. If legal advice or other expert assistance is required, the services of a competent professional person should be sought.
　　— From a *Declaration of Principles* jointly adopted by a Committee of the American Bar Association and a Committee of Publishers and Associations

This book is available at quantity discounts for bulk purchases.
For information, call 1-800-872-5627.

Contents

Foreword

It wasn't until I started researching the material for this book that I realized how many people have been or will be affected by poor credit. Over 1.7 million people will file for bankruptcy in this country alone, and there are millions more whose credit has been damaged to one degree or another. I myself am one of the millions who have been affected by damaged credit. Prior to writing this book, I spent three years as financial manager for a large automobile franchise looking at thousands of credit reports to determine if a customer qualified for a loan. I would say, without hesitation, over ninety percent of the credit reports I looked at were damaged to some degree by negative credit. The final determinant that drove me to create this resource was the people. Looking at a piece of paper is one thing; however, meeting face-to-face with the person(s) whose credit has been decimated is another. Time after time, customers would ask me to help them fix their credit, and all I could do was tell them to be responsible and pay their bills. Responding in that manner may sound callous; however, it was all I really knew. In time I realized it wasn't always due to irresponsibility that a person's credit was damaged. Sometimes life just takes an unfortunate turn, and among other areas in life, one's credit suffers. After having this paradigm shift, I knew there was a way I could help, and I knew people wanted to be helped. I have written this book to assist people in getting back on their feet as responsible credit consumers. I hope that the information in this book will point you in the direction of achieving stronger credit and a better way of living.

Chapter 1

Welcome

IT'S YOUR CREDIT

One of the most important things to remember regarding credit problems is that you're not alone. Millions of good, hard-working people all around the country are currently having or have had problems with their credit. However, your awareness of the importance of having good credit has put you one step closer to actually achieving a good credit rating and improving your quality of living.

Even though your credit rating may seem like an intangible asset, it is one of the most valuable and important assets that you have. Without a good credit rating your financial, occupational, and personal goals are at risk of being severely limited. In order to obtain the privilege of using a credit card, your credit rating is checked. If a company determines your credit to be unsatisfactory, you will be denied. From the moment you are denied, your quality of living is impeded. If you can't get a credit card, you can't rent a car, order tickets, or even rent a video. Because your credit rating was determined to be unsatisfactory, most companies will not let you use their money.

Today more than ever, many businesses perform routine background checks during the hiring process. Once again, if your credit rating reveals something of concern to them, you can be turned away for employment. Since maintaining a good credit rating is important in today's society, a poor credit rating can have a negative snowball effect toward your personal goals. Good, strong credit allows you to live with financial security and enables you to purchase items without depleting your life savings.

Repairing your credit can seem like a monumental task; however, it can also be as easy as writing a letter or making a phone call. Your decision to repair your credit rating will benefit you for the rest of your life.

The more time you invest now toward strengthening your credit rating, the better your quality of life will be.

WHAT INFORMATION DOES THIS BOOK CONTAIN?

The Complete Guide to Credit Repair has been written to assist you in repairing and strengthening your credit rating. This guide provides you with step-by-step instructions, explanations, situations, details, testimony, inserts, and prewritten letters that will help you repair and strengthen your credit rating. After reading this guide, you will have a good understanding of the following items:

1. How credit works and how it affects you
2. How credit agencies operate
3. How to establish your credit report
4. What lenders are looking for
5. How to read a credit report and how to get a copy of your report
6. What credit problems can arise
7. How to determine your credit problems
8. How to strengthen your credit rating
9. How to write letters, and where to send those letters
10. How to follow through on what you start

HOW TO GET STARTED

Once you finish reading the material, you will begin the process of repairing and strengthening your credit. Before beginning the process, you must follow some important procedures in order to keep your information well organized. Following this set of procedures will help develop your organization skills, along with increasing your chances of strengthening your credit. The next section will detail these procedures.

HOW TO STAY ORGANIZED

1. Write your goals—what you plan to achieve—on the insert provided. Creating goals will help you stay focused on an end result and expedite the strengthening process (pages 5, 165 and 167).

2. Retrieve all of your old financial records. The more records you can find, the better your chances of providing vital background information when necessary.

3. Save all of your current financial records, especially the major records (e.g., billing statements, cancelled checks, and receipts). Use a typewriter or a computer when creating letters. (If you do not have access to a typewriter or a computer, you can print the letters in black ink.)

4. If you have access to a computer, save all of the letters you create on a disk.

5. Make photocopies of your financial records and any documents you send.

6. Clearly state the terms and conditions on any agreements, whether oral or written. Anything that you and the creditor or credit agency agree upon must be put in writing and signed, with both parties receiving copies.

7. Send all letters by certified mail. Certified mail enables you to obtain a receipt. Keeping records of your transactions is important.

8. When sending any type of payment, always pay by check or money order. Using a check or money order allows you to have an instant receipt of your payment.

HOW TO USE THE SAMPLE LETTERS

The Complete Guide to Credit Repair provides you with 67 letters that have been prepared to get results and to save you time and money. Each letter has been carefully written to coincide with its corresponding section or topic (e.g., Letter #1 coincides with getting a free, yearly copy of your credit report).

After you have finished reading a section, a letter will be assigned for you to use, if applicable. Be sure you use the letter that corresponds with the section you are working on. Do not interchange letters unless otherwise instructed.

The letters are presented in three separate appendices, according to the order in which the letters will be sent. Table 1.1 shows how the three categories are broken down and where each letter can be found, according to its number. Reproduce the letters using your computer. When reproducing the letter, you should quote word for word, only changing the personal information.

Appendix	Contents of Appendices	Letters Contained
A	Original Letters	(1–22)
B	Follow-Up Letters	(23–46)
C	Final Follow-Up Letters	(47–67)

(Table 1.1)

HOW TO USE THE INSERTS

The Complete Guide to Credit Repair also contains fourteen inserts that provide you with an organized format in which you can pass along important information. Each insert has been carefully written to coincide with its corresponding section and letter (e.g., Insert "G" accompanies Letter #11). Not all letters have an accompanying insert.

The inserts are all presented in one separate appendix. After you finish reading a section, an insert will be assigned for you to use, if applicable. Be sure you use the insert that corresponds to the section you are dealing with.

When completing an insert, you should carefully read the entire insert and be absolutely positive the information you provide is correct. Using false or incorrect information is not only going to slow down the strengthening process, but the misrepresentation of information is also illegal.

Here is an easy reference chart (Table 1.2) that will help you match the correct insert(s) with its corresponding letter.

Insert Letter*	Description
A	Goal Writing
B	Credit Clinic Offers
C	Revise Your Goals
D,E,F	Letter #10
G	Letter #11
H	Letters #12, #13, #14, & #15
I	Letters #14 & #15
J	Letters #20 & #13
K	Letter #17
L	Letter #18
M	Letter #19
N	Letter #16

(Table 1.2)

*Some of the inserts are used by more than one sample letter.

WRITE OUT YOUR GOALS

Creating goals is one of the most crucial steps you will take as you proceed through the process of repairing your credit situation. Without goals, your sense of direction can easily become clouded, leading to outcomes other than the ones you desire.

You have without a doubt set many goals during your lifetime, such as making a sports team, achieving good grades in school, earning a raise at work, or cleaning that cluttered basement. Goal setting is important; however, just as important is the type of goal you set. A goal that provides you with the best opportunity for success is one that is reachable, measurable, and time sensitive.

Designing a goal around these three principles is the key to good goal setting. A reachable goal is one that can be realistically achieved. For example, let's say you are trying to get a raise. You are currently earning $35,000 a year; however, you feel you are worth at least $50,000. When you go into negotiations, you know where you want to be. You don't have an unrealistic figure such as $100,000 in your head, nor will you be thinking too low, such as $39,000. As an obtainable goal, $50,000 a year is a very reachable and a realistic goal.

Staying with the same example, once you realistically set the parameters for your goal, you now have something to use as a yardstick to measure your progress. When you negotiate your raise, you can immediately measure how successful you were at achieving your desired outcome.

The third characteristic of a goal that provides you the opportunity for success is making the goal time sensitive. A goal must have a beginning and an end. Setting up a time line for your goal allows you to accurately track the progress of your goal. And by tracking your goal, you are able to see how close you are to achieving what you set out to achieve based on a unit of measurement.

When developing your first set of goals, to accurately encompass the areas you are attempting to correct, you should keep the goals broad. Incorporate all of the areas you are concerned about in this first goal-writing exercise. At this stage it is important not to limit yourself. The more areas you are able to determine that need attention, the greater your percentage of success. You will have another opportunity to further revise your goals, narrowing them down to better focus on the areas that are of most importance to you and your credit repair needs.

For now, use Insert A to list the goals that you would like to attain. In order to help you write your goals, let's take a look at some examples of goals that are general, reachable, measurable, and time sensitive:

Example Goals:

I, (Your Name), want to strengthen my credit report by adding accounts which are not reporting to my credit report by (date).

I, (Your Name), want to strengthen my credit report by deleting any old account from my credit report by (date).

I, (Your Name), want to strengthen my credit report by deleting any old inquiries from my credit report by (date).

The information contained within this book is set up to help you achieve a stronger credit rating. By following the steps outlined in this chapter, you better your chances of reaching your goals.

Chapter 2

Credit???

What is "credit"? *The American Heritage College Dictionary* lists several definitions for the word *credit*. Each of the definitions listed holds a key to unlocking the true meaning behind the importance of credit, as it relates to the consumer. Credit is defined as "a reputation for sound character or quality—standing; influence based on the good opinion or confidence of others; reputation for solvency and integrity entitling a person to be trusted in buying or borrowing; an arrangement for deferred payment of a loan or purchase; and the time allowed for deferred payment."

In many cases your reputation and character as a consumer are determined by how people perceive your past credit experiences. People who let you use their money want some kind of reassurance that they will be paid back. The people who let you use their money to purchase goods need some measure to help them determine your reputation for solvency and integrity. If a person is going to buy or borrow, they must be able to show why they should be trusted with the other person's money.

The measurements used to determine whether a person may be trusted to use someone else's money is where many of us run into trouble. The practice of lending and borrowing are common in our society. Nobody thinks twice about charging large amounts on credit. And the only time we think about what we have charged is when we have to pay the bill at the end of the month. Once the bill arrives two things can happen: one, the bill gets paid on time with no problems; or two, for one reason or another the bill does not get paid on time or does not get paid at all. If the bill gets paid late or not at all, along with your feelings of guilt, your troubles are compounded by agencies whose job it is to keep track of your payment histories. Just about every consumer move we make today is watched and recorded by someone. So, just who is watching over us, and why?

WHO'S WATCHING ME?

In today's society good credit is the cornerstone to financial wellness. Without the security of having good credit, you are placing yourself at a big disadvantage. Many of the primary and recreational purchases made are done so using credit: homes, cars, televisions, boats, and motorcycles—just to name a few. If you have experienced any financial problems, such as bankruptcy, foreclosure, repossession, or just late payments, your ability to purchase these primary and recreational items using credit is severely restricted.

Why is your ability to purchase using credit severely restricted when you have experienced credit difficulties? There are businesses called *consumer reporting agencies* (credit agencies) that keep a very close watch over you.

Consumer reporting agencies are businesses whose primary function is to, legally, gather and report your credit information. Companies and organizations through which you are trying to obtain credit use information from these agencies, about you, to make credit decisions.

So, you may ask yourself why and how all of this vast information is gathered and how it affects you. Both are good questions, to which many people do not know the answers. Let's take a closer look at how credit agencies gather and use your credit information.

WHERE DOES THE INFORMATION COME FROM?

There are thousands of credit agencies located throughout the United States. A credit agency's main function is to gather information on you and put that information into a report called a *credit report* or a *consumer report*. A credit report is a document that contains a factual record of an individual's consumer credit payment history. The report is generated by the credit agency, and is just one of the pieces of information used by a third party to determine an individual's credit worthiness. We should note here for the future that a credit report is different from a consumer file. A *consumer file* is a collection of all of the information gathered on an individual by a credit agency. Your credit report is a permanent part of your consumer file.

The *Fair Credit Reporting Act* is a piece of legislation that governs what credit agencies can and can't access. The Fair Credit Reporting Act, *15 U.S.C. 1681a(d),* states that "a credit report must bear on a consumer's credit worthiness, credit standing, credit capacity, character, general reputation, personal characteristics, or mode of living." So, by definition credit agencies have a wide spectrum from which they can gather information on you. It is important to remember that every aspect of your consumer life and certain areas of your private life are accessible to the credit agencies. An example of the type of information a credit agency can place in your credit file and on your credit report is the practice of writing bad checks. The writing of a bad check reflects on your overall reputation. If a business reports the writing of a bad check to a credit agency, the credit agency has the right to place that information in your consumer file and on your credit report.

Since you know what types of information the credit agencies can gather, you now need to know from whom they can receive the information. Credit agencies gather the information they need from businesses, organizations, public and private sources, and governmental offices. These are the same businesses, organizations, public and private sources, and governmental offices that you use on a daily basis. The credit agencies solicit places of business, promising complete and accurate credit information— this is how a credit agency is judged. Once a place of business is signed up with a credit agency, the two share information about you that is vital to both of them. All of the groups solicited by the credit agencies rely upon the completeness and accuracy of the information gathered to help them in decisions involving an individual's credit worthiness.

WHO ARE THE THREE MAIN CREDIT AGENCIES?

There are three main consumer reporting agencies: *Trans-Union, Equifax,* and *Experian* (formerly known as TRW). These three major information agencies have a lock on the credit reporting industry and sum up more than 90 percent of the credit report information in the United States. Because all three agencies are competing with one another for the same customer base, they are extremely competitive with one another, and do not share information. Competition has driven these agencies to expand their regions. The agencies now provide information to subscribers throughout the world. The agencies are profit oriented, with profits coming from the individuals and businesses who subscribe to them as their source for consumer information.

It is important to remember that a consumer reporting agency is judged on the thoroughness, timeliness, and accuracy of the consumer information it gathers. The fact that the agencies do not share information with one another is both a blessing and a curse. For example, if one report shows all good accounts, you are in good shape. However, if another report shows a bad account, you are in trouble. Many businesses and organizations subscribe to more than one credit reporting agency to avoid making costly errors in judging a person's credit worthiness.

As explained briefly before, the agencies get businesses and organizations to subscribe to them by proving that their credit reports and credit files are the most accurate and complete information available on the consumer (you and me). The best credit agency is the one that reports both negative and positive information with timeliness and accuracy. Businesses and organizations rely heavily upon the timeliness and accuracy of the information when attempting to make a qualified decision regarding credit worthiness.

Credit agencies are supposed to report factual information regarding your background information and consumer credit habits. Since credit agencies begin reporting your background information and consumer credit habits from your first credit experience, it is important to establish or re-establish a solid consumer foundation early on. However, establishing and re-establishing is not always an easy task to undertake. Knowing where to turn and what to look for is key to starting off on the right foot. So you ask, how do I establish or re-establish myself as a responsible credit-using consumer? Let's take a look at just a few ideas that can be beneficial to you as a responsible credit consumer.

Chapter 3

How to (Re-)Establish Your Credit Rating

Regardless of whether you are just beginning to enter the world of credit or are starting to rebuild your credit, you need to find ways to establish yourself as a responsible consumer. When establishing or re-establishing your credit, you should start small. Being able to stay within your credit bounds is an important key to establishing yourself as a responsible consumer. Over-extending yourself while trying to get established will only increase the likelihood of putting you back to square one, and you only get so many chances. Because the process of establishing or re-establishing credit can be frustrating, knowing what to do can help lessen the frustration. When looking to establish or re-establish your credit, there are many different options available. Let's take a look at some of them.

PAY YOUR CURRENT BILLS ON TIME

The most important part you play in maintaining a good credit rating is paying your monthly bills on time. By paying your current bills on time, you will help to ensure that your current accounts remain as positive marks on your credit report. Regardless of any past negative accounts you may have, your present, 6- to 12-month habits are the most crucial. Since creditors look for patterns, by eliminating late payments and nonpayments, you will show the creditors that you can pay your monthly bills on time. Soon after, you will have the credit grantors coming to you.

OPEN A CHECKING AND SAVINGS ACCOUNT

If you do not have a checking and or a savings account, open one. Although checking and savings account information are not reported to the credit agency directly, the accounts do provide creditors with information on the way you manage your finances. A checking account will provide you with cancelled checks—certified evidence that you pay your bills, such as rent, utilities, and small loans. A savings account will allow you to show creditors the amount of money you have available in the case of an emergency. Checking and saving accounts are not only smart financial tools for your use, but also good tools that help your would-be creditors make a credit decision.

APPLY FOR SECURED CREDIT CARDS

Whether you have bad credit or no credit at all, you may have found it difficult to obtain a credit card. Many creditors do not feel comfortable giving credit to people who have bad credit or no credit. One way you can help establish a positive credit rating is applying for a secured credit card.

A secured credit card works much in the same manner as an unsecured credit card: you have a line of credit that you are responsible for, and you make payments each month on the balance you have acquired. Just like unsecured credit cards, secured credit cards carry interest rates, finance charges, application fees, annual fees, and available lines of credit. However, there are differences between the two. To get a secured credit card, you deposit money into an account or a Certificate of Deposit, which is specifically set aside as collateral for use of the credit card. Once your money is in the account, you use the secured credit card the same way you would use any other credit card. Your money will remain in the account until you either close your account or seriously default on your payments.

Your line of credit with a secured credit card is a direct percentage of the amount of money you deposit. Most institutions allow you to charge anywhere from 50 to 100 percent of the amount you deposit. The average minimum deposit required has been figured at around $300. When deciding how much money to use as a deposit, 5 percent of your annual income is a good sound figure. The following chart (Table 3.1) will give you a quick reference for how much money you should deposit.

Annual Income	Multiply By .05	Amount of Deposit
$12,000	.05	$600
$18,000	.05	$900
$24,000	.05	$1,200
$36,000	.05	$1,800
$42,000	.05	$2,100
$50,000	.05	$2,500

(Table 3.1)

As stated previously, a secured credit card works the same as an unsecured credit card. Even though you deposit money into an account, you are responsible for making monthly payments on anything charged to your account. There are a few additional issues you should be aware of when applying for a secured credit card.

Do They Report to a Credit Agency?

First and foremost, does the institution to which you are applying for your secured credit card report to a credit agency? Because the main reason behind having a secured credit card is to establish or re-establish your credit rating, you must be sure to apply to a secured credit card institution that reports their information to the credit agencies. Whether you use the card or not, the account should show up on your credit report as a good, month-to-month account. You want to belong to an institution that does *not* report the information as secured. Be sure to ask whether or not the institution to which you are applying follows this practice.

How to Choose the Best Cards

There are hundreds of firms offering secured credit cards. In order to find the best card for your purposes, you are going to have to do your homework. Before committing to a secured credit card, you need to determine the reasons you are applying. You should try to find a secured credit card that will best match your current financial situation.

In general, secured credit cards carry higher interest rates and annual fees than on unsecured credit cards. The range on interest rates can be anywhere from 13.0 to 22.0 percent. Just as a lower rate is beneficial when using an unsecured credit card, the same holds true for a secured credit card. The finance charges are based on a percentage of what you have charged to the account—depending on the interest rate. As for the application fee, certain institutions charge a one-time fee, ranging from $20 to $80, which is usually nonrefundable (regardless of your acceptance or denial). And almost all institutions assess an annual fee, ranging from $20 to $80 (once approved for the card).

All reputable institutions that offer secured credit cards pay you interest on the amount you have deposited as collateral. The average interest rate paid on the amount you have deposited is 1 to 4 percent. Finding out how much a lender is paying in interest becomes critical, as the amount you put down as collateral grows.

Finally, because the main reason behind using a secured credit card is to establish your credit, keeping a balance is important. The longer you are able to demonstrate good consumer habits, the stronger your credit rating will become and your credit worthiness will grow. Keeping an account open 12 to 24 months will help strengthen your credit rating.

How to Keep an Eye Out for Scams

Be careful to watch out for secured credit card scams. Because many deceptive people understand how important credit is in our society, these people will try to take advantage of others with credit problems. Beware of such things as:

- **"900" Numbers:** If you have to call a "900" number, you are most likely being charged unnecessary phone charges. You could end up paying hundreds of dollars for useless phone calls.
- **Unspecified or Misleading Information:** Many times you can avoid being scammed by reading carefully or asking the right questions. Some not-so-reputable companies will purposely leave out important information regarding deposit amounts, application fees, and processing fees. Others will deliberately mislead you by using the old "bait and switch" method. They place an ad asking you to apply for a regular "gold" secured credit card, but when you get the card you are only allowed to purchase items from a particular catalog offering items at an exorbitant amount. So, be leery of lenders who advertise their secured cards as "gold" cards.

- **Credit Clinic Offers:** Some so-called credit repair clinics, credit card consultants, or credit repair companies offer secured credit cards. When dealing with these individuals or firms, DO NOT hand over any money until you ask all of the right questions. Remember, time and responsible consumer spending habits are the best way to strengthen your credit. A high-priced credit repair clinic can, legally, do no more than you can do with the right information.

Insert B, found in Appendix D, contains questions you should ask before applying for a secured credit card or dealing with a credit clinic. Once you have asked the right questions, you can determine which secured credit card is right for you.

The best place to obtain a secured credit card is at your local bank, credit union, or another reputable institution. For a complete list of programs offering secured credit cards, call or write to the following:

Name of Service	Where To Write	Fee	Telephone Number
CardTrak of America	Secured Card Report Box 1700 Frederick, MD 21702	$10.00	(800) 874-8999
BankCard Holders of America	Secured Credit Card List BHA Customer Service 524 Branch Drive Salem, VA 24153	$4.00	N/A

(Table 3.2)

APPLY FOR LOW-BALANCE CREDIT CARDS

Once again, since a lender may be reluctant to give you an unsecured, high-balance credit card, you may have a better chance applying for a low-balance credit card. A lender may take a chance, granting you a credit card; however, they start you off with a low, rather than a high credit limit. The card might start off with a $200 or $300 limit. Eventually, your credit limit should be raised, depending on how responsibly you make your monthly payments.

APPLY FOR DEPARTMENT STORE CREDIT CARDS

A great place to go when trying to establish or re-establish your credit is the local shopping mall. Large department store chains usually have their own financing, which is available to the public. Department stores' credit guidelines tend to be less strict. Most department stores will qualify you for a certain credit limit based on several criteria, usually job, income, and credit history.

A credit limit of $100 is all you need to begin strengthening your credit. Once you purchase an item using the store's credit, you turn around and make several monthly payments. Because most large department stores report to a credit agency, your monthly payments will be recorded on your permanent credit history (be sure to ask a representative of the store if their credit card payments are reported to a credit bureau). As long as you act responsibly and make your payments on time, your credit rating will become stronger. Remember, the same holds true regarding overspending when you are using a department store credit card. Only spend as much as you can afford.

FIND SOMEONE TO COSIGN WITH YOU

Because of your lack of credit or your bad credit, you can ask someone to cosign for you. A good co-signer is someone who has good, established credit. The cosigner's main function is to get you, as a responsible credit user, up and running. You can ask a parent, sibling, relative, friend, or acquaintance to be a cosigner. Some lenders require the cosigner to be a family member; others do not. However, in the event you default on your financial obligation, the lender can go after the cosigner for full payment and can report the negative information to both your and the cosigner's credit report. So be sure to fulfill your responsibilities; otherwise your cosigner will be after you, as well as your creditors.

## Chapter 4

Getting a Copy of Your Credit Report

Before you can begin straightening out your credit, you have to know how to acquire a copy of your credit report. Depending on your situation, there are several reasons why you would want to obtain a copy of your credit report. Table 4.1 lists some reasons for ordering your credit, broken down into three areas, as well as the corresponding request letter:

Area	Reason	Sample Letter
1	Just checking your information (Free Yearly)	#1
	Just checking your information (Small Fee)	#2
2	Denied Credit (Free)	#3
	Denied Employment (Free)	#4
	Denied Insurance (Free)	#5
	Denied Rental Housing (Free)	#6
3	Unemployed (Free)	#7
	A victim of fraud (Free)	#8
	On public assistance (Free)	#9

(Table 4.1)

WHEN YOU ARE JUST CHECKING YOUR INFORMATION

To ensure the integrity of your credit report, you should check at least once a year, if not every six months, to make sure the information reported is up-to-date and correct.

Unfortunately, as of March 1, 1997, credit agencies no longer automatically provide a complimentary credit report. Today most credit agencies charge a nominal processing fee. Check the "Cost by State" section in Table 4.2 to see if your state is listed. If your state is not listed, you must pay the required general fee. If your state is listed, you should refer to Table 4.3 to find the applicable fee for requesting your credit report. Some state's regulations still require credit agencies to provide a complimentary credit report, once a year, upon request, for residents who reside in those states. Table 4.3 will show you whether or not your state's regulations provide that you be able to request a complimentary copy of your credit report.

Agency Contact Information and Fees

Agency	Address	Web Address	Phone Number	Cost by State
Trans-Union	Trans-Union Corporation Consumer Disclosure Center P.O. Box 390 Springfield, PA 9064-0390	www. transunion.com	(800) 888-4213	All states $8.00 except: CT, CO, GA, MA, ME, MD, NJ, VT, Virgin Islands
Experian	Experian National Consumer Assistance Center P.O. Box 2104 Allen, TX 75013-2104	www. experian.com	(888) 397-3742	All states $8.00 except: CT, CO, GA, HI, IL, ME, MA, MD, NJ, NM, NY, PA, SC, SD, TX, VT, DC, WV
Equifax	Equifax Information Service Center P.O. Box 740241 Atlanta, GA 30374-0241	www. equifax.com	(800) 997-2493	All states $8.00 except: CT, CO, GA, ME, MD, MA, NJ, VT

(Table 4.2)

You can order a copy of your credit report by sending the corresponding sample letter or contacting the credit agency by phone or Internet. To ensure that you receive the most up-to-date and accurate information, contact the credit agency directly.

STATE & COST OF OBTAINING CREDIT REPORT

Trans-Union	Experian	Equifax
Connecticut, $5 each request	Connecticut, $5.30 for first request, $7.95 for additional requests	Connecticut, $5 each request
Colorado, Free once a year, $8 for additional request	Colorado, Free once a year, $8 + (.28 for Denver Res.) for additional requests	Colorado, Free once a year, $8 for additional requests
Georgia, Free once a year, $8 for additional requests	Georgia, Free once a year, $8 for additional requests	Georgia, Free once a year, $8 for additional requests
Maine, $2 each request	Maine, $2 each request	Maine, $3 each request
Maryland, Free once a year, $8 for additional requests	Maryland, Free once a year, $5.25 for additional requests	Maryland, Free once a year, $5 for additional requests
Massachusetts, Free once a year, $8 for additional requests	Massachusetts, Free once a year, $8 for additional requests	Massachusetts, Free once a year, $8 for additional requests
New Jersey, Free once a year, $8 for additional requests	New Jersey, Free once a year, $8 for additional requests	New Jersey, Free once a year, $8 for additional requests
Vermont, Free once a year, $8 for additional requests	Vermont, Free once a year, $7.50 for additional requests	Vermont, Free once a year, $7 for additional requests
Virgin Islands, $1 each request	Hawaii, $8.32 each request	
	Illinois, $8 + ($.48 for Chicago residents)	
	New Mexico, $8.46 each request	
	New York, $8.66 each request	
	Pennsylvania, $8.56 each request	
	South Carolina, $8.32 each request	
	South Dakota, $8.32 each request	
	Texas, $8.66 each request	
	Washington D.C., $8.46 each request	
	West Virginia, $8.48 each request	

(Table 4.3)

WHEN YOU ARE DENIED CREDIT, EMPLOYMENT, INSURANCE, OR RENTAL HOUSING

You are entitled to a complimentary copy of your credit report from an agency when their report is used to determine any of the following:

1. Denial for any type of credit within the last 60 days.
2. Denial for employment within the last 60 days.
3. Denial for personal insurance within the last 60 days.
4. Denial for rental housing within the last 60 days.

You can receive your complimentary credit report by contacting the credit agencies by phone or Internet or by sending the corresponding letters, as shown in table 4.4.

Agency	Address	Web Address	Phone Number	Cost
Trans-Union	Trans-Union Corporation Consumer Disclosure Center P.O. Box 390 Springfield, PA 9064-0390	www.transunion.com	(800) 888-4213	Free
Experian	Experian National Consumer Assistance Center P.O. Box 949 Allen, TX 75013-0949	www.experian.com	(888) 397-3742	Free
Equifax	Equifax Information Service Center P.O. Box 740241 Atlanta, GA 30374-0241	www.equifax.com	(800) 997-2493	Free

(Table 4.4)

WHEN YOU ARE UNEMPLOYED, A VICTIM OF FRAUD, OR ON PUBLIC ASSISTANCE

You are entitled to a complimentary copy of your credit report if you can show that you fall into any one of the following categories:

1. You are unemployed and plan to seek employment within 60 days.
2. You are a victim of credit fraud.
3. You are a recipient of any type of public assistance.

You can receive your complimentary credit report by contacting the credit agencies by phone or Internet or by sending the corresponding letters, as shown in table 4.5.

Agency	Address	Web Address	Phone Number	Cost
Trans-Union	Trans-Union Corporation Consumer Disclosure Center P.O. Box 390 Springfield, PA 9064-0390	www.transunion.com	(800) 888-4213	Free
Experian	Experian National Consumer Assistance Center P.O. Box 9530 Allen, TX 75013-0949	www.experian.com	(888) 397-3742	Free
Equifax	Equifax Information Service Center P.O. Box 740241 Atlanta, GA 30374-0241	www.equifax.com	(800) 997-2493	Free

(Table 4.5)

You now have the information you need to go ahead and request a copy of your credit report from the appropriate agencies. Requesting a copy of your credit report from each of the three major credit agencies is a good idea. Ordering and comparing the information on all three reports will help ensure the accuracy of the information documented on your credit report.

Once determining the reason for requesting a copy of your credit report, you should find the appropriate corresponding letter. Each of the nine situations given for requesting a copy of your credit report has a corresponding letter (see table 5.1). The letters are found in Appendix A. Find the correct letter, fill in the information needed, and send it out.

Even if you decide to order your report by phone or via the Internet, you should fill out the information so you have it handy. Taking the time to fill out the insert beforehand can save you the aggravation of passing along incorrect information. Incorrect information can and will slow down the request process.

The letters contain all of the information needed by the credit agencies to process your request. However, if you are requesting a free report, you must send a copy of your documentation that entitles you to a free copy (e.g., letter showing the denial of credit.) The only other additional information that needs to be sent is a copy of your driver's license and a copy of your most recent utility bill for identification purposes.

Chapter 5

What's on My Credit Report?

Being able to read and understand the information listed on your credit report is a critical part of strengthening your credit rating. Legally, your credit report is allowed to contain information concerning your credit worthiness, credit standing, credit capacity, general character, general reputation, personal characteristics, and mode of living.

The three major credit reports compiled by different agencies are basically broken down in the same manner, each with small differences in their order and content. Tables 5.1, 5.2, and 5.3 show the breakdown of the sections:

Trans-Union
1 General Information
2 Summary Line
3 Public Records
4 Account Information or Trades
5 List of Inquiries
6 Consumer Statement (Optional)

Table 5.1

Equifax
1 Personal Identification Information
2 Public Records Information
3 Collection Agency Account Information
4 Credit Account Information
5 Additional Information
6 Companies That Requested Credit File

Table 5.3

Experian
1 How to Read This Report
2 Your Credit History
3 Your Credit History Was Reviewed By
4 Please Help Us Help You
5 Identification Information

Table 5.2

Within each of the above sections, credit agencies enter information that help businesses make qualified decisions regarding your credit worthiness, credit standing, credit capacity, general character, general reputation, personal characteristics and mode of living.

A detailed breakdown of each of the three major credit agency's credit report is provided in the following sections. The sections are broken down exactly as they appear on each respective credit report. And each begins with an excerpt from the complete credit report, which is found at the end of the section. Below each excerpt is a brief explanation of the section and a quick reference chart that explains in greater detail the bolded categories.

TRANS-UNION CREDIT REPORT

General Information

TRANS UNION CREDIT REPORT (1)				
FOR	MRT/SUB (2)	IN FILE (3)	DATE (4)	TIME (5)
(90000)	6CH	8/77	04/27/96	16:59CT
RPT (6)		SSN (7)	DOB (8)	
SMITH, MARY A.		000-00-0000	11/50	
-BROWN, MARY A.				
CURR/ADD (9)		RPTD (10)	TEL# (11)	
5000 MADE UP AVE., ANYTOWN, IL 60006		05/93	435-0000	
FRMR/ADD (12)				
1000 MAIN ST., WALKING, IL 60001		07/88	333-3333	
1700 SOUTH BLVD., MOONTOWN, MA 46533				
CURR EMP & ADD (13)	PSTN/INCM (14)		EMPDATE RPTD(15)	
WIDGET INC.	SUPERVISOR		07/88	
ANYTOWN, IL				
FRMR EMP & ADD (16)				
SELF EMPLOYED	SELF		09/78	

The "General Information" section is the first section of the Trans-Union credit report. The General Information section's function is to provide vital background information used for identification purposes. The information is divided into sixteen categories, which are listed and defined as follows:

Number	Abbreviation	Description
1	TRANS-UNION CREDIT REPORT	Lists the name of the credit agency responsible for supplying the credit report.
2	MRT/SUB	Lists the code used by the credit agency and business.
3	IN-FILE	Lists the date information was first entered into the credit report.
4	DATE	Lists the date when the credit report was requested and run.
5	TIME	Lists the time when the credit report was requested and run.
6	RPT	Lists your full name (sometimes previous names and aliases are located underneath).
7	SSN	Lists your social security number.
8	DOB	Lists your date of birth.
9	CURR/ADD	Lists your current place of residency along with address.
10	RPTD	Lists the date showing the amount of time you have been at your current place of residency and former place(s) of residency.
11	TEL#	Lists the telephone number that is listed for your address.
12	FRMR/ADD	Lists your former place(s) of residency along with addresses.
13	CURR EMP & ADD	Lists your current place of employment along with addresses.
14	PSTN/INCM	Lists your position within your place of employment.
15	EMPDATE RPTD	Lists the date when you began working for your current employer and former employer(s).
16	FRMR EMP & ADD	List your former place(s) of employment along with addresses.

(17)	(18)	(19)	(20)	(21)	(22)	(23)
TRD=8	NEG=5	PUB=3	COL=3	INQS=5	BAL=$113.4K	HC-CL=140K-90K

The "Summary Line" section is located between the General Information and the Public Records sections. The Summary Line section's function is to give an overview of the type of information listed in the other sections of the credit report and to give you a summary of the gross dollar amounts you have in credit. The information is divided into seven categories, which are listed and defined as follows:

Number	Abbreviation	Description
17	TRD	Lists the number of accounts on your credit report.
18	NEG	Lists the number of negative accounts on your credit report.
19	PUB	Lists the number of accounts located in the public records section.
20	COL	Lists the number of accounts that have been turned over to a collection agency.
21	INQS	Lists the number of credit reports pulled and viewed by subscribers to the credit agency.
22	BAL	Lists the current dollar balance of open accounts.
23	HC/CL	Lists two figures, your high credit limit and your credit limit. High Credit means the amount of credit you have accumulated over time. Credit Limit means the amount of credit that you have available for use.

Public Records

(24) SOURCE	(25) COURT	(26) DATE	(27) LIAB	(28) TYPE	(29) ASSETS	(30) PAID	(31) DOCKET NUM.	(32) PLAINTIFF/ATTORNEY
Z34000001	DC	03/89	$54.2K	7X	$3000	01/90	9231045	MR. JONES
CHAPTER 7 BANKRUPTCY DISCHARGED								
Z34000002	SC	06/87	$7000	CJ		10/87	00011LM2700	
CIVIL JUDGMENT								
Z34000003	FE	04/91	$2500	PF		07/91	91111400	
PAID FEDERAL TAX LIEN								

The "Public Records" section is located directly after the Summary Line section. The Public Records section contains information that pertains to legal issues such as bankruptcies, civil judgments, federal and state tax liens, along with any other issues that have been handled through the legal system or a government agency. The information in the Public Records section is divided into nine categories, which are listed and defined as follows:

Number	Abbreviation	Description
24	SOURCE	Lists the source code for the public record. The source code is determined by the credit agency for their records.
25	COURT	Lists the type of court from which the public record originated such as: **CC:** County Clerk's Office **CT:** County Court **DC:** District Court **FE:** Federal District Court **SC:** Small Claims Court
26	DATE	Lists the date the public record was reported.
27	LIAB	Lists the amount of liability you are responsible for.
28	TYPE	Lists the type of public record reported such as: **7X:** Chapter 7 Bankruptcy **13X:** Chapter 13 Bankruptcy **CJ:** Civil Judgment **PF:** Paid Federal Tax Lien **SC:** Small Claims Court
29	ASSETS	Lists the amount of assets involved.
30	PAID	Lists the date the public record account was satisfied and paid.
31	DOCKET NUM	Lists the case docket number assigned by the court.
32	PLAINTIFF/ATTORNEY	Lists the plaintiff's or attorney's name.

Account Information

	(33) (34) SUB.NAME/ACCT#	(36) (37) SUB#/TERM	(38) OPND	(39) HICR	(40) (41) DVER/CLS	(42) BAL/MAX	(43) DEL	(44) (45) PAY.PAT/HIST	(46) MOP
Line 1	SLMA/LSCK V (35)	6101010	10/91	$2000	10/92A	$0	$0	N/A	I09
Line 2	(34) 50008887770K	(37) M24			(41) 09/92F				
Line 3	(47) I					(48) * TRANSFER/ STUDENT LOAN			
	THE CAR BANK Q 277100046893 M	2534332 60M275	05/86	$11.6K	03/89A 03/89C * BANKRUPTCY /REPOSSESSION AUTOMOBILE	$9500	$9500	N/A	I08
	VISA 8 I	6202020	04/87	$3000	02/96A 03/89C * BANKRUPTCY /CREDIT CARD	$3000	$3000	N/A	R09
	ARMOR SYSTEMS Y I	2150030	11/92	$625	03/96A 11/92F * PLACED FOR COLLECTION	$625	$625	N/A	09B
	BIG CITY MORTG Q 913211006428 C	4625314 360M875	04/85	$90.0K	03/89A 03/89F * BANKRUPTCY/ FORECLOSURE	$79.0K	$0	N/A	M05
	JEWELRY STORE J I	722BX34	12/93	$700 $900	05/96A / CHARGE ACCOUNT	$325	$0	(44) 11111111111X 11111111111 (45) 24V 0 0 0	R01
	GRT AUTO BANK B 132152500033650 I	276S154 60M325	06/94	$22.0K	05/96A / AUTOMOBILE	$19.6K	$0	11111111111 11111111111 23V 0 0 0	I01
	BANCHOUSE Q 9136421876 I	24163215 360M725	12/92	$78.0K	05/96A / FHA LOAN	$64.0K	$0	11111111111 11111111111 24V 0 0 0	M01

The "Account Information" section is located between the Public Records section and the Inquiry section. The Account Information section's function is to provide a detailed listing of the status of all credit transactions, beginning from your first experience as a consumer using credit. The "Account Information" section is where the bulk of the credit information is located and where creditors place the greatest importance when making a decision regarding credit worthiness. The "Account Information" section is broken down into 16 categories. In order to make the credit report easier to read, we have broken the report down further into three information lines. The categories are listed and defined as follows:

Line 1 of the Trans-Union credit report:

Number	Abbreviation	Description
33	SUB. NAME	The name of the business with which you have the account.
35	N/A	The account classification symbol assigned by the credit agency.
36	SUB#	The special code assigned to the account by the credit agency.
38	OPND	The date the account was first opened.
39	HICR	The original or beginning balance of the account.
40	DVER	The date of the last time the account was reported to the credit agency by the place of business.
42	BAL	Lists the current amount owed on the account at the time the account was required.
43	DEL	Lists the dollar amount that is reported as being delinquent.
44	PAY.PAT	Lists the month-to-month history of payments on the account as reported by the place of business, and recorded in the following code: **X:** The information for that period was not reported. If the information was not reported, one of two things may have happened. One, the agency did not record the information, or two, the subscriber did not turn in the information. Neither reflects negatively toward you. **1:** The account was reported and is currently on time (your ultimate goal is to have all 1's on your credit report.) **2:** The account was reported and is currently or was at least 30 days past its due date. **3:** The account was reported and is currently or was at least 60 days past its due date. **4:** The account was reported and is currently or was at least 90 days past its due date. **5:** The account was reported and is currently or was at least 120 days past its due date.

Line 1 of the Trans-Union credit report: — cont.

Number	Abbreviation	Description
46	TYPE OF ACCOUNT/MOP	Lists the type of account, showing what type of credit agreement was entered into between the consumer and the creditor. It also lists the current account rating or the Method of Payment (MOP) showing the status of how the account is being paid or not being paid. The account rating is recorded with the following code:

TYPE

C: Check Credit (Line of Credit)
I: Installment Account (Finite number of payments)
M: Mortgage Account
O: Open Account (Balance is due every 30, 60, or 90 days)
R: Revolving or Option Account (Payment varies from month to month depending on the balance.)

MOP

UR: An unrated account, just like a nonrated account.
00: A nonrated account—the information is not reported.01: An account that is paid on time and in good standing.
02: An account that is more than 30 days past its due date—not in good standing.
03: An account that is more than 60 days past its due date—not in good standing.
04: An account that is more than 90 days past its due date—bad standing.
05: An account that is more than 120 days past its due date—very bad standing.
07: An account that has gone bad; however, a payment plan has been established by the customer and business and/or collection agency.
08: An account that has been placed in repossession and the item in question has been repossessed.
09: An account that is considered to be a Bad Debt, Collection, or a Charge-Off. The account was never paid and the business most likely wrote the account off as a loss.

Line 2 of the Trans-Union credit report:

Number	Abbreviation	Description
34	ACCT#	Lists the account number assigned to that piece of credit from the original credit grantor.
37	TERM	Lists the length of time the loan is carried, usually followed by the amount due each month.
41	CLS	Lists the date when the account was closed, either by the consumer or the credit grantor.

Line 3 of the Trans-Union credit report:

Number	Abbreviation	Description
47	N/A	Lists the Equal Credit Opportunity Act account designators. The type of account is determined by the number of people who have signed for the credit. There are several ways in which an account can be listed. The following codes are used by the credit agency. **I:** An individual account, with only one user **C:** A cosigned account **A:** A cosigned account, with an Authorized User **M:** A cosigned account, with the Primary User liable for the account **P:** A Shared Account, but not a C or an A account **U:** An Undesignated Account **T:** A relationship with an account is terminated
48	N/A	Lists the description of the type of loan for the credit line.
45	HIST	Lists the summary of the History of Payments made on the account: **Column 1:** The number of months the account has been reported to the credit bureau. **Column 2:** The number of payments that have been 30 days late. **Column 3:** The number of payments that have been 60 days late. **Column 4:** The number of payments that have been 120 days late.

List of Inquiries

(49) INQR	7		
(50) DATE	**(51) ECOA**	**(52) SUBCODE**	**(53) SUBNAME**
4/11/96	I	_____	CAREXPO
5/31/95	I	_____	NPC/FST
5/31/95	C	_____	LPC/HTC
6/12/94	I	_____	GRT AUTO BK
3/09/94	I	_____	CRDT CHECK
2/12/94	C	_____	MASTER CRD
2/01/93	I	_____	JEWL

The "List of Inquiries" section is located between the Account Information section and the Consumer Statement section. The List of Inquiries section's function is to provide a detailed listing of subscribers who have requested to view your credit report. The List of Inquiries section is divided into five categories. The categories are listed and defined as follows:

Number	Abbreviation	Description
49	INQR	Lists the number of times your credit report has been requested.
50	DATE	Lists the date the subscriber requested your credit report.
51	ECOA	Lists the Equal Credit Opportunity Act account designators. Refer back to number 47 from the Account Information section to see the different codes.
52	SUBCODE	Lists the code given to the inquiry by the credit agency.
53	SUBNAME	Lists the names of subscribers who have requested your credit report.

Consumer Statement

(54) CONSUMER STATEMENT:	THE REPOSSESSION TO THE CAR BANK WAS DUE TO A DIVORCE. I'M LISTED AS THE PRIMARY SIGNER; HOWEVER, MY EX-WIFE GOT THE CAR AND DID NOT MAKE THE PAYMENTS. THE SAME HOLDS TRUE FOR THE MORTGAGE WITH BIG CITY MORTGAGE.

** END OF CREDIT REPORT**
REPORT SERVICES BY:

Trans-Union Sample Credit Report

Now that each section of the credit report has been broken down and explained, let's take a look at what the entire Trans-Union credit report looks like with all of the sections in place. The information and numbering contained in this complete credit report is the same as in each of the individual sections discussed earlier.

(33) (34) SUB.NAME/ACCT#	(36) (37) SUB#/TERM	(38) OPND	(39) HICR	(40) (41) DVER/CLS	(42) BAL/MAX	(43) DEL	(44) (45) PAY.PAT/HIST	(46) MOP
SLMA/LSCK V (35)	6101010	10/91	$2000	10/92A	$0	$0	N/A	I09
(34) 50008887770K	(37) M24			(41) 09/92F				
(47) I				(48) * TRANSFER/ STUDENT LOAN				
THE CAR BANK Q	2534332	05/86	$11.6K	03/89A	$9500	$9500	N/A	I08
277100046893	60M275			03/89C				
M				* BANKRUPTCY /REPOSSESSION AUTOMOBILE				
VISA 8	6202020	04/87	$3000	02/96A	$3000	$3000	N/A	R09
				03/89C				
I				* BANKRUPTCY /CREDIT CARD				
ARMOR SYSTEMS Y	2150030	11/92	$625	03/96A	$625	$625	N/A	09B
				11/92F				
I				* PLACED FOR COLLECTION				
BIG CITY MORTG Q	4625314	04/85	$90.0K	03/89A	$79.0K	$0	N/A	M05
913211006428	360M875			03/89F				
C				* BANKRUPTCY/ FORECLOSURE				
JEWELRY STORE J	722BX34	12/93	$700 $900	05/96A	$325	$0	(44) 1111111111X 11111111111 (45)	R01
I				/ CHARGE ACCOUNT			24V 0 0 0	
GRT AUTO BANK B	276S154	06/94	$22.0K	05/96A	$19.6K	$0	11111111111 11111111111	I01
132152500033650	60M325							
I				/ AUTOMOBILE			23V 0 0 0	
BANCHOUSE Q	24163215	12/92	$78.0K	05/96A	$64.0K	$0	11111111111 11111111111	M01
9136421876	360M725							
I				/ FHA LOAN			24V 0 0 0	

(49)
INQR   7

(50) DATE	(51) ECOA	(52) SUBCODE	(53) SUBNAME
4/11/96	I	_____	CAREXPO
5/31/95	I	_____	NPC/FST
5/31/95	C	_____	LPC/HTC
6/12/94	I	_____	GRT AUTO BK
3/09/94	I	_____	CRDT CHECK
2/12/94	C	_____	MASTER CRD
2/01/93	I	_____	JEWL

(54)
CONSUMER STATEMENT: THE REPOSSESSION TO THE CAR BANK WAS DUE TO A DIVORCE. I'M LISTED AS THE PRIMARY SIGNER,   HOWEVER, MY EX-WIFE GOT THE CAR AND DID NOT
                                        MAKE THE PAYMENTS THE SAME HOLDS TRUE FOR THE MORTGAGE WITH BIG CITY MORTGAGE.

** END OF CREDIT REPORT**
REPORT SERVICES BY:

EQUIFAX CREDIT REPORT

Personal Identification Information

(1)	Call this number with questions - (800) 000 - 0000
(2)	Request Reference: WEBWCP1111111110000000
	(3) Report Date: 27 April 1996

CREDIT PROFILE for Mary Smith

Personal Identification Information

Mary A. Smith (4)

5000 MadeUp Ave. (5)

Anytown, IL 60006

Previous Address(es) (6)

   1000 Main St., Walking, IL 60001

   1700 South Blvd., Moontown, MA 46533

SSN   000-00-0000 (7)

DOB   04 November 1950 (8)

Last Reported Employment: (9)   Self Employed

Public Record Information

(10)   (11)   (12)   (13)   (14)

Bankruptcy filed on 03/1989 in City of Chicago with case or other ID number 0987654321 With liabilities of $54,200,

(15)   (16)   (17)   (18)

assets of $3,000, exempt amount of $25,000 Type of Personal, filed Individual

(19)

Status - Voluntary Chapter 7

(20)

Satisfied Judgment filed on 04/1987 in City of Chicago with a case or other ID number 0987654321, filed by Plaintiff

(21)   (22)   (23)

against Defendant for the amount $7,000 with status Satisfied on 10/1987 and verified on 11/1987.

(24)

Lien filed on 04/1991 in the City of Chicago with case or other ID number 0987654321 for the amount of $2,500,

(25)

Released on 10/1987 and Verified on 12/1987.

The "Personal Identification Information" section is the first section of the Equifax credit report. The Personal Identification Information in this section comes from your creditors, providing vital background information used for identification purposes. The information is divided into nine categories, which are listed and defined as follows:

Number	Abbreviation	Description
1	QUESTIONS	Lists the number given to call if you have any questions regarding your credit report.
2	REQUEST REFERENCE#	Lists the number given to use as a reference when dealing with the credit agency.
3	REPORT DATE	Lists the day the credit report was requested and run.
4	YOUR NAME	Lists your full name.
5	CURR/ADD	Lists your current place of residency along with address.
6	FRMR/ADD	Lists your former place(s) of residency along with address(es).
7	SSN	Lists your social security number.
8	DOB	Lists your date of birth.
9	LAST REPORTED EMPLOYMENT	Lists your last place of employment that was reported to the credit agency.

Public Records Information

Public Record Information

(10) (11) (12) (13) (14)
Bankruptcy filed on 03/1989 in City of Chicago with case or other ID number 0987654321 With liabilities of $54,200,
(15) (16) (17) (18)
assets of $3,000, exempt amount of $25,000 Type of Personal, filed Individual
(19)
Status - Voluntary Chapter 7

(20)
Satisfied Judgment filed on 04/1987 in City of Chicago with a case or other ID number 0987654321, filed by Plaintiff
(21) (22) (23)
against Defendant for the amount $7,000 with status Satisfied on 10/1987 and verified on 11/1987.

(24)
Lien filed on 04/1991 in the City of Chicago with case or other ID number 0987654321 for the amount of $2,500,
(25)
Released on 10/1987 and Verified on 12/1987.

The "Public Records Information" section is located directly after the Personal Identification Information section. The Public Records section contains information that pertains to legal issues such as bankruptcies, civil judgments, federal and state tax liens, or any issues that have been handled through the legal system or a government agency. The information in the Public Records section is divided into sixteen categories, which are listed and defined as follows:

Number	Abbreviation	Description
10	TYPE	Lists the type of public record reported.
11	DATE	Lists the date the public record was reported.
12	PLACE	Lists the city in which the public record was filed.
13	CASE/ID NUMBER	Lists the case docket or ID number assigned by the court.
14	LIABILITIES	Lists the amount of liability that you are responsible for.
15	ASSETS	Lists the amount of assets involved.
16	EXEMPT	This is only for a bankruptcy and lists the amount that is not covered under a bankruptcy.
17	TYPE	This is only for a bankruptcy and lists the type of bankruptcy acquired.
18	FILED	Lists how the bankruptcy was filed, either individual or joint.
19	STATUS	Lists the type of bankruptcy and its status.
20	PLAINTIFF / ATTORNEY	Lists the plaintiff's or attorney's name.
21	AMOUNT	Lists the amount of money the plaintiff requests.
22	(UN)SATISFIED	Lists the date the public record account was satisfied and paid.
23	VERIFIED	Lists the date when the status of the public record was verified by the credit agency.
24	AMOUNT	Lists the amount of money owed on the lien.
25	RELEASED	Lists the date on which the lender reported the lien as released.

Collection Agency Account Information

```
Collection Agency Account Information
            (26)                        (27)
   Collection Agency Name      Phone - (000) 555-1212
                 (28)                     (29)              (30)             (31)
      Collection reported 11/1992 and assigned to Collection Agency Name on 11/1992 by Your Creditor for account
                 (32)                       (33)                  (34)            (35)        (36)
      number 0987654321 which is an Individual Account for the amount of $625 with a balance $625 with status in
                                            (37)
      Bankruptcy and last activity on 01/1986.
```

The "Collection Agency Account Information" section is located between the Public Records Information section and the Credit Account Information section. The Collection Agency Account Information section's function is to list all accounts that have been turned over to a collection agency. The Collection Agency Account Information section is divided into thirteen categories. The categories are listed and defined as follows:

Number	Abbreviation	Description
26	COLLECTION AGENCY NAME	Lists the name of the collection agency to which the delinquent account was turned over.
27	PHONE	Lists the telephone number of the collection agency.
28	DATE	Lists the date the collection account was reported to the credit agency.
29		Lists the name of the collection agency to which the delinquent account was turned over.
30	DATE ASSIGNED	Lists the date on which the account was assigned to the collection agency.
31	CREDITORS NAME	Lists the name of the creditor who turned the account over to the collection agency.
32	ACCOUNT NUMBER	Lists the account number assigned by the creditor.
33	ECOA TYPE	Lists the ECOA account designator (explained on page 212).
34	AMOUNT	Lists the beginning dollar amount the creditor turned over to the collection agency.
35	BALANCE	Lists the current balance of the account held by the collection agency.
36	STATUS	Lists the current status of the collection account, such as "open" or "closed."
37	LAST ACTIVITY	Lists the date of the last change in the account's status.

(38) Company Name	(39) Account Number (40) Whose Account	(41) Date Opened	(42) Date of Last Activity	(43) Type of Account (44) and Status	(45) High Credit	Items as of Date (46) Terms	(47) Balance	(48) Past Due	Reported (49) Date Reported
SLMA/LSCK	50008887770K Individual Account	10/91	10/92	Installment	2000	24M	0		10/92
(50) Student loan-payment deferred									
THE CAR BANK	277100046893 Shared Account	05/86	03/89	Installment 90-120 days past due	11600	60M	9500	9500	04/89
VISA	Individual Account	04/87	02/96	Revolving 60 - 89 days past due	3000		3000	3000	03/96
(51) Prior Paying History 30 days past due 2 times; 60 days past due 1 time; 90 + days past due 1 time 08/1989 - 30 - 59 days past due 10/1989 - 90 - 119 days past due 12/1988 - 60 - 89 days past due									
BIG CITY MORTG Real estate mortgage	913211006428 Joint Account	04/85	03/89	Installment	90000	360	79000		04/89
JEWELERY STORE Charge	Individual Account	12/93	05/96	Revolving	700		325		05/96
GRT AUTO BANK Auto loan	132152500033650 Individual Account	06/94	05/96	Installment Pays as agreed	22000	60M	19600		05/96
BANCHOUSE Real estate mortgage	9136421876 Individual Account	12/92	05/96	Installment Pays as agreed	78000	360	64000		05/96

The "Credit Account Information" section is located between the Collection Agency Account Information section and the Additional Information section—assuming that section is on your credit report. The Credit Account Information section's function is to provide a detailed listing of your credit transactions, beginning from your first experience as a consumer using credit. This section is where the bulk of the credit information is located and where the creditors place the greatest importance when making a decision regarding your credit worthiness. The Credit Account Information section is divided into fourteen categories. The categories are listed and defined as follows:

Number	Abbreviation	Description
38	COMPANY NAME	Lists the name of the business with whom you have the account.
39	ACCT#	Lists the account number assigned to that piece of credit from the original credit grantor.
40	WHOSE ACCOUNT	Lists the Equal Credit Opportunity Act account designators. The type of account is determined by the number of people who have signed for the credit. There are several ways in which an account can be listed. The following codes are used by the credit agency. **I:** An Individual Account, with only one user **C:** A Cosigned Account **J:** A Joint Account **A:** A Cosigned Account, with an Authorized User **B:** On behalf of another person **M:** A Cosigned Account, with the Primary User liable for the account **S:** A Shared Account, but not a C or an A account **U:** An Undesignated Account **T:** A relationship with an account terminated
41	DATE OPENED	Lists the date the account was first opened.
42	DATE OF LAST ACTIVITY	Lists the date the last time the account was reported as being active (e.g., payment or change).
43	TYPE OF ACCOUNT	Lists the type of account, showing what type of credit agreement was entered into between the consumer and the creditor such as: **C:** Check credit (line of credit) **I:** Installment account (finite number of payments) **M:** Mortgage account **O:** Open account (balance is due every 30, 60 or 90 days) **R:** Revolving or Option account (payment varies from month to month depending on the balance)
44	STATUS	Lists how the account is being paid or not being paid.
45	HIGH CREDIT	Lists the original or highest amount owed on the account.
46	TERMS	Lists the length of time the loan is to be carried, usually followed by the amount due each month.
47	BALANCE	Lists the current amount owed on the account at the time the account was reported.
48	PAST DUE	Lists the dollar amount that is reported as being delinquent.
49	DATE REPORTED	Lists the date the account was last reported to the credit report.
50	N/A	Lists the type of credit; also gives additional notes.
51	PRIOR PAYING HISTORY	The first line lists the number of times the account has been either 30, 60, or 90 plus days past due. The second line lists the dates of the two most recent delinquencies, plus the date of the most severe delinquency.

Additional Information

Additional Information
Foreclosure reported on 03/1989 by Big City Mortgage Co. verified 04/1985

The "Additional Information" section is located between the Credit Account Information section and the Companies That Requested Your Credit File section. The Additional Information section's function is to list other miscellaneous types of credit-related information. If there is any information listed in this section, the information should be self-explanatory.

Companies That Requested Your Credit File

Companies that Requested your Credit File			
(52) 11 Apr 1996	**(53)** Car Expo	12 Sep 1995	Credit Check
31 May 1995	NPC / FST	02 Feb 1994	Master Card
31 May 1995	LPC / HTC	10 Apr 1994	Great Auto Bank
07 Aug 1995	Sears	11 Apr 1994	Great Auto Bank

The "Companies That Requested Your Credit File" section is located at the end of the credit report. This section's function is to provide a detailed listing of subscribers who have requested to view your credit report. The section is divided into two categories. The categories are listed and defined as follows:

Number	Abbreviation	Description
52	DATE	Lists the date the subscriber requested to view your credit report.
53	BUSINESS NAMES	Lists the names of the subscribers who have requested to view your credit report.

Equifax Sample Credit Report

Now that each section of the credit report has been broken down and explained, let's take a look at what the entire Equifax credit report looks like with all of the sections in place. The information and numbering contained in this complete credit report is the same as in each of the individual sections discussed earlier.

Collection Agency Account Information

(26) (27)
Collection Agency Name   Phone - (000) 555-1212

(28)   (29)   (30)   (31)
Collection reported 11/1992 and assigned to Collection Agency Name on 11/1992 by Your Creditor for account

(32)   (33)   (34)   (35)   (36)
number 0987654321 which is an Individual Account for the amount of $625 with a balance $625 with status in

(37)
Bankruptcy and last activity on 01/1986.

Credit Account Information

(38) Company Name	(39) Account Number (40) Whose Account	(41) Date Opened	(42) Date of Last Activity	(43) Type of Account (44) and Status	(45) High Credit	Items as (46) Terms	of Date (47) Balance	Reported (48) Past Due	(49) Date Reported
SLMA/LSCK	50008887770K Individual Account	10/91	10/92	Installment	2000	24M	0		10/92
(50) Student loan-payment deferred									
THE CAR BANK	277100046893 Shared Account	05/86	03/89	Installment 90-120 days past due	11600	60M	9500	9500	04/89
VISA	Individual Account	04/87	02/96	Revolving 60 - 89 days past due	3000		3000	3000	03/96
(51) Prior Paying History	30 days past due 2 times; 60 days past due 1 time; 90 + days past due 1 time 08/1989 - 30 - 59 days past due 10/1989 - 90 - 119 days past due 12/1988 - 60 - 89 days past due								
BIG CITY MORTG	913211006428 Joint Account	04/85	03/89	Installment	90000	360	79000		04/89
Real estate mortgage									
JEWELERY STORE	Individual Account	12/93	05/96	Revolving	700		325		05/96
Charge									
GRT AUTO BANK	132152500033650 Individual Account	06/94	05/96	Installment Pays as agreed	22000	60M	19600		05/96
Auto loan									
BANCHOUSE	9136421876 Individual Account	12/92	05/96	Installment Pays as agreed	78000	360	64000		05/96
Real estate mortgage									

Additional Information

Foreclosure reported on 03/1989 by Big City Mortgage Co. verified 04/1985

Companies that Requested your Credit File

(52)	(53)			
11 Apr 1996	Car Expo	12 Sep	1995	Credit Check
31 May 1995	NPC / FST	02 Feb	1994	Master Card
31 May 1995	LPC / HTC	10 Apr	1994	Great Auto Bank
07 Aug 1995	Sears	11 Apr	1994	Great Auto Bank

END OF PROFILE

EXPERIAN CREDIT REPORT

Explanatory Information

```
This is your consumer identification        ID#  1234561234          (1)
number.  Please refer to this number
when you call or write.


        MARY A. SMITH
        5000 MADE UP AVE.          (2)
        ANYTOWN, IL  60006


HOW TO READ THIS REPORT:

EXPERIAN IS THE INDEPENDENT COMPANY FORMED FROM TRW'S INFORMATION SERVICES BUSINESS.   (3)

AN EXPLANATORY ENCLOSURE ACCOMPANIES THIS REPORT.  IT DESCRIBES YOUR CREDIT RIGHTS AND OTHER HELPFUL
INFORMATION.  IF THE ENCLOSURE IS MISSING, OR YOU HAVE QUESTIONS ABOUT THIS REPORT, PLEASE CONTACT THE
OFFICE LISTED ON THE LAST PAGE.

AS PART OF OUR FRAUD-PREVENTION PROGRAM, ACCOUNT NUMBERS MAY NOT FULLY DISPLAY ON
THIS REPORT.
        (4)
```

The "Explanatory Information" section is the first section of the Experian credit report. This section's function provides you with details of how to read the credit report, what to do if information is missing, and who to contact. This section also brings to your attention Experian's practice of not fully displaying account numbers as a part of the company's fraud-prevention program.

Number	Abbreviation	Description
1	ID NUMBER	Lists the identification number assigned to the credit report and file. You should refer to this number whenever you contact the credit agency regarding your credit questions.
2	NAME & ADDRESS	Lists the name and address of the individual for whom the credit report was generated.
3	N/A	Lists the type of information you should have received with your copy of your credit report. If you have any questions, this section indicates the correct office to contact.
4	N/A	Lists information regarding Experian's fraud-prevention program. The account numbers may not be displayed in full on your credit report.

Your Credit History Information

YOUR CREDIT HISTORY: (5)

THIS INFORMATION COMES FROM PUBLIC RECORDS OR ORGANIZATIONS THAT HAVE GRANTED CREDIT TO YOU. AN ASTERISK BY AN ACCOUNT INDICATES THAT THIS ITEM MAY REQUIRE FURTHER REVIEW BY A PROSPECTIVE CREDITOR WHEN CHECKING YOUR CREDIT HISTORY. IF YOU BELIEVE ANY OF THE INFORMATION IS INCORRECT, PLEASE LET US KNOW.

The "Credit History Information" section is located between the Explanatory Information section and the Reviewed By Information section. This section provides a detailed listing of all your credit transactions and public records—beginning from your first experience as a credit-using consumer.

In order to help understand the information better, this section has been broken down into two areas: "Public Record Information" and "Account History Information." The Public Record Information area details all legal issues that have gone through a court of law. The Account History Information area provides detailed records of your credit accounts.

Number	Abbreviation	Description
5	YOUR CREDIT HISTORY	Lists an explanation of where the information listed in your credit history comes from and what accounts may need further review.

Public Record Information

ACCOUNT	DESCRIPTION
(6) 1 *US BKPT CT IL (7) 201 W WILSON STREET CHICAGO IL 60006 (8) DOCKET # 9231045	(9) (10) VOLUNTARY BANKRUPTCY CHAPTER 7 DISCHARGED ON 01/10/90. (11) (12) (13) PETITIONED ON 08/12/89. RECORDED ASSETS: $3,000, LIABILITIES: $54.200. (14) YOU ARE SOLELY RESPONSIBLE FOR THIS PUBLIC RECORD ITEM.
2 *SUING COUNTY COURT PROFITS CNTY CT HOUSE CHICAGO IL 60023 DOCKET # 00011LM2700	(15) (16) (17) SMALL CLAIMS CIVIL JUDGMENT SATISFIED ON 10/24/87. ORIGINAL FILING (18) (19) (14) DATE 06/13/87. AMOUNT: $7000. PLAINTIFF: TOM AND JERRY. YOU ARE SOLEY RESPONSIBLE FOR THIS PUBLIC ITEM.
3 *COOKED COUNTY FEDERAL COURT P O BOX 000 CHICAGO IL 60606 CERTIFICATE # 91111400	(20) (21) (14) FEDERAL TAX LIEN ON 04/04/91. AMOUNT: $2500. YOU ARE SOLELY RESPONSIBLE FOR THIS PUBLIC RECORD ITEM.

Number	Abbreviation	Description
6	COURT	Lists the name of the court where the public record originated.
7	COURT ADDRESS	Lists the address of the court where the public record originated.
8	DOCKET/CERTIFICATE NUMBER	Lists the case docket or certificate number assigned to the bankruptcy by the court.
9	BANKRUPTCY TYPE	Lists the type of bankruptcy filed for through the courts.
10	BANKRUPTCY STATUS	Lists whether or not the bankruptcy has been discharged by the court.
11	PETITIONED	Lists the date when the bankruptcy was officially petitioned through the court.
12	RECORDED ASSETS	Lists the amount of assets involved.
13	LIABILITIES	Lists the amount of the liability.
14	RESPONSIBILITY	Lists the amount the court deems as your responsibility.
15	CIVIL JUDGMENT TYPE	Lists the type of civil judgment filed through the court.
16	CIVIL JUDGMENT STATUS	Lists whether or not the civil judgment has been satisfied through the court's eyes.
17	ORIGINAL FILING DATE	Lists the date when the civil judgment was officially filed through the court.
18	CIVIL JUDGMENT AMOUNT	Lists the amount the court holds as your responsibility.
19	PLAINTIFF	Lists the Plaintiffs involved with the civil judgment.
20	LIEN TYPE	Lists the type of lien filed through the court.
21	LIEN AMOUNT	Lists the amount the court holds as your responsibility.

Account History Information

ACCOUNT	DESCRIPTION

4
(22)
*SMLA/LSCK
(23)
P O BOX 444
MISSING YOU IL 60607
(24)
BANKING
(25)
ACCT #
50008887XXXX

(26)   (27)   (28)
THIS EDUCATION LOAN WAS OPENED 10/20/91 AND HAS 120 MONTH REPAYMENT
(29)
TERMS. YOU HAVE CONTRACTUAL RESPONSIBILITY FOR THIS ACCOUNT AND ARE
(30)   (31)
PRIMARILY RESPONSIBLE FOR ITS PAYMENT. ORIGINAL AMOUNT: $2000.

(32)   (33)   (34)   (35)
AS OF 10/14/92, THIS ACCOUNT IS PAID. PREVIOUSLY WAS 90 DAYS PAST DUE. ORIGINAL DELINQUENCY
(36)
DATE 05/12/92. MONTHS REVIEWED: 12

5 VISA
P O BOX 700
BEDROCK IL 68880
BANKING
ACCT #
80110078911XXXX

THIS CREDIT CARD ACCOUNT WAS OPENED 04/09/87 AND HAS REVOLVING
REPAYMENT TERMS. YOU HAVE CONTRACTUAL RESPONSIBILITY FOR THIS ACCOUNT
AND PRIMARILY RESPONSIBLE FOR ITS PAYMENT. HIGH BALANCE: $3000

THIS CLOSED ACCOUNT IS 180 DAYS PAST DUE AND WAS 90 DAYS PAST DUE 2 OTHER TIME. SCHEDULED MONTHLY
PAYMENT: $50. LAST PAYMENT REPORTED TO EXPERIAN: 02/28/92. BALANCE: $3,000 ON 02/12/96. PAST DUE: $635.
MONTHS REVIEWED: 72.
(37)
PAYMENT HISTORY: 654321111111111111111-------
(38)
TIMES LATE: 30=1, 60=0, 90+=2
** CREDIT LINE CLOSED - GRANTOR REQUEST - REPORTED BY SUBSCRIBER **
(39)
Balance History: Between 10-90 and 02-96 your credit limit was $3000. Between 04-87 and 03-89 your credit limit was $2800. Your balance was:

6 GREAT AUTO BANK
757 BUMPER AVENUE
HEADLIGHT IL 60690
FINANCE
ACCT #
13215250003XXXX

THIS AUTOLOAN WAS OPENED 06/16/94 AND HAS 60 MONTH REPAYMENT TERMS.
YOU HAVE CONTRACTUAL RESPONSIBILITY FOR THIS ACCOUNT AND ARE PRIMARILY
RESPONSIBLE FOR ITS PAYMENT. ORIGINAL AMOUNT: $22,000.

AS OF 05/12/95, THIS OPEN ACCOUNT IS CURRENT AND ALL PAYMENTS ARE BEING MADE ON TIME. SCHEDULED
MONTHLY PAYMENT: $325. LAST PAYMENT REPORTED TO EXPERIAN: 05/08/96. BALANCE $19,450 ON 05/15/96. MONTHS
REVIEWED: 24.
(39)
Balance History: The original amount of this account was $22,000. Your balance was:

04/15/96 - $19600,	03/15/96 - $19750,	02/15/96 - $19900,	01/15/96 - $20050,
12/15/96 - $20200,	11/15/95 - $20350,	10/15/95 - $20500,	09/15/95 - $20650,
08/08/96 - $20800,	07/07/95 - $20950,	06/07/95 - $21100,	05/07/95 - $21250,
04/07/95 - $21400,	03/07/95 - $21550,	02/07/95 - $21700,	01/08/95 - $21850,
12/15/94 - $22000.			

Number	Abbreviation	Description
22	NAME OF ACCOUNT	Lists the name of the business with whom you have the account.
23	ADDRESS OF ACCOUNT	Lists the address of the business with whom you have the account.
24	TYPE OF BUSINESS	Lists the type of industry of the business with whom you have the account.
25	ACCOUNT NUMBER	Lists the account number assigned to that piece of credit from the original credit grantor.
26	TYPE OF CREDIT	Lists the type of credit agreement you have entered into with the credit grantor.
27	OPENED	Lists the date the account was first opened.
28	TERM	Lists the length of time the loan is to be carried, usually followed by the amount due each month.
29	RESPONSIBILITY	Lists whether or not you signed a contract holding you responsible for making payments.
30	ECOA ACCOUNT DESIGNATOR	Lists the Equal Credit Opportunity Act account designators. The type of account is determined by the number of people who have signed for the credit (explained on page 212).
31	ORIGINAL AMOUNT	Lists the beginning balance of the account before any payments were made.
32	AS OF DATE	Lists the "as of date," which is the date when the account was reported as being closed or last reported as being open.
33	ACCOUNT STATUS	Lists whether the account is being paid or is delinquent.
34	PAST DUE	Lists whether or not the account is delinquent, and if delinquent, the number of days past due.
35	DELINQUENCY	Lists the first time the account was reported as being past due.
36	MONTHS REVIEWED	Lists the number of times the account has been reviewed by the credit agency.

Number	Abbreviation	Description
37	PAYMENT HISTORY	Lists a running month-to-month summary of how your account is being paid. Read from left to right. The first number, letter, or mark refers to the balance date that has been reported. The payment history is recorded using the following codes: **1:** An account that is more than 30 days past its due date. **2:** An account that is more than 60 days past its due date. **3:** An account that is more than 90 days past its due date. **4:** An account that is more than 120 days past its due date. **5:** An account that is more than 150 days past its due date. **6:** An account that is more than 180 days past its due date. **7:** An account that is reported as being derogatory. **8:** An account that is reported as being _____. **9:** An account that is reported as being _____. **C:** An account that is reported as being current. **0:** An account that is reported as being current or having a zero balance. **N:** An account that is reported as having a zero balance (not reported that month.) **B:** An account that is reported being changed (e.g., from open to closed.) **(Dash):** An account that is reported as having no payment history for that month.
38	TIMES LATE	Lists the number of times the account has been either 30, 60, or 90 days past due.
39	BALANCE HISTORY	Lists the balance of your account on a month-to-month basis.

Your Credit History Was Reviewed By

YOUR CREDIT HISTORY WAS REVIEWED BY:

THE FOLLOWING INQUIRIES ARE REPORTED TO THOSE WHO ASK TO REVIEW YOUR CREDIT HISTORY.

INQUIRY	DESCRIPTION
(41)	(44) (45)
8 CAR EXPO CENTER	03 / 11 / 96 INQUIRY MADE FOR EXTENSION OF CREDIT, REVIEW OR
(42)	OTHER PERMISSIBLE PURPOSE.
123 WEST CEDAR	
THE TOWN IL 60670	
(43)	
FINANCE	
9 NPC / FST	05 / 31 / 95 INQUIRY MADE FOR EXTENSION OF CREDIT, REVIEW OR
P O BOX 4500	OTHER PERMISSIBLE PURPOSE.
WISHINGTON DC 88809	
BANKING	
10 LPC / HTC	05 / 31 / 95 INQUIRY MADE FOR EXTENSION OF CREDIT, REVIEW OR
101 CLEAVER STREET	OTHER PERMISSIBLE PURPOSE.
BUTCHER IL 60606	
FINANCE	
11 SEARS ROEBUCK & CO.	08 / 07 / 95 INQUIRY MADE FOR EXTENSION OF CREDIT, REVIEW OR
1000 SOUTH AVENUE	OTHER PERMISSIBLE PURPOSE.
ESTATES HOFFMAN IL 60607	
FINANCE	

THE FOLLOWING INQUIRIES ARE NOT REPORTED TO THOSE WHO ASK TO REVIEW YOUR CREDIT HISTORY. THEY ARE INCLUDED SO THAT YOU HAVE A COMPLETE LIST OF INQUIRIES. (46)

INQUIRY	DESCRIPTION
12 CREDIT CHECK	09 / 12 / 95 INQUIRY MADE FOR PRESCREEN PROGRAM. YOUR FILE
P O BOX 1234	WAS MATCHED AGAINST THIS CREDITOR'S CRITERIA TO DEVELOP
SIMPLE TOWN WI 48756	A LIST OF NAMES FOR A CREDIT OFFER OR SERVICE.
NATL CREDIT CARDS	
13 MASTER CARD	02 / 02 / 94 INQUIRY MADE FOR PRESCREEN PROGRAM. YOUR FILE
23 GRAND CANYON DRIVE	WAS MATCHED AGAINST THIS CREDITOR'S CRITERIA TO DEVELOP
BIG HOLE OH 34567	A LIST OF NAMES FOR A CREDIT OFFER OR SERVICE.
NATL CREDIT CARDS	
14 GREAT AUTO BANK	04 / 10 / 94 INQUIRY MADE FOR PURPOSES OF ACCOUNT REVIEW.
765 CHESTER AVENUE	
FRONT SEAT IL 60697	
FINANCE	
15 JEWEL FOOD SERVICES	04 / 11 / 94 INQUIRY MADE FOR PURPOSES OF ACCOUNT REVIEW.
1000 LETTUCE STREET	
FROZEN IL 60687	

The "Your Credit History Was Reviewed By" section, also known as "Inquiries," is located between the Your Credit History section and the Please Help Us Help You section. This section provides a detailed listing of subscribers who have requested your credit report and the reason(s) for their request. This section has six categories, which are listed and defined as follows:

Number	Abbreviation	Description
41	NAME	Lists the names of the subscribers who have requested your credit report.
42	ADDRESS	Lists the address of the subscribers who have requested your credit report.
43	BUSINESS TYPE	Lists the industry type of the business that requested to view your credit report.
44	DATE	Lists the date the subscriber requested to view your credit report.
45	REASON	Lists the explanation behind why your credit report was reviewed.
46	OTHER	Lists the other subscribers who requested a copy of your credit report; however, these inquiries only show up on your own personal credit report.

Please Help Us Help You

PLEASE HELP US HELP YOU: (47)

AT EXPERIAN WE KNOW HOW IMPORTANT YOUR GOOD CREDIT IS TO YOU. IT IS EQUALLY IMPORTANT TO US THAT OUR INFORMATION BE ACCURATE AND UP TO DATE. LISTED BELOW IS THE INFORMATION YOU GAVE US WHEN YOU ASKED FOR THIS REPORT. IF THE INFORMATION IS NOT CORRECT OR YOU DID NOT SUPPLY US WITH YOUR FULL NAME, ADDRESS FOR THE PAST 5 YEARS, SOCIAL SECURITY NUMBER AND YEAR OF BIRTH, THIS REPORT MAY NOT BE COMPLETE. IF THIS INFORMATION IS INCOMPLETE OR NOT ACCURATE, PLEASE LET US KNOW.

YOUR NAME: (48)   MARY A SMITH   SOCIAL SECURITY #: (51) 000-00-0000
                                                        DATE OF BIRTH: (52) 11 / 05 / 1950

ADDRESS: (49)   5000 MADE UP AVE   SPOUSE: (53) N/A
                       ANYTOWN IL 60006

OTHER ADDRESSES: (50) 1000 MAIN STREET
                       WALKING IL 60001

The "Please Help Us Help You" section is located between the Your Credit History Was Reviewed By section and the Identification Section. This section helps ensure the information you provided to the credit agency when ordering your credit report is correct. The credit agency lists the information in order to give you the opportunity to double-check its accuracy. The section has seven categories, which are listed and defined as follows:

Number	Abbreviation	Description
47	N/A	Lists an explanation of what information is to come.
48	YOUR NAME	Lists the complete name you provided to the credit agency.
49	ADDRESS	Lists the current address you provided to the credit agency.
50	OTHER ADDRESSES	Lists the additional address(es) you provided to the credit agency.
51	SOCIAL SECURITY NUMBER	Lists the social security number you provided to the credit agency.
52	DATE OF BIRTH	Lists the date of birth you provided to the credit agency.
53	SPOUSE	Lists the name of your spouse, if any, you provided to the credit agency.

Identification Information

IDENTIFICATION INFORMATION:

THE FOLLOWING ADDITIONAL INFORMATION HAS BEEN PROVIDED TO US BY ORGANIZATIONS THAT REPORT INFORMATION TO US.

SOCIAL SECURITY #:   000-00-0000 REPORTED 10 TIMES.
(54)

DRIVERS LICENSE #:   IL 60050050577
(55)   LAST REPORTED 3 / 96

ADDRESSES: (56)   5000 MADE UP AVENUE
                     ANYTOWN IL 60006-7869 GEOGRAPHICAL CODE=78-987600-7
  (57)
THIS SINGLE FAMILY DWELLING ADDRESS WAS FIRST REPORTED 6/93 AND LAST REPORTED 3/96 BY UPDATE. LAST REPORTED BY BANCHOUSE. ADDRESS REPORTED 7 TIMES.

                     1000 MAIN STREET
                     WALKING IL 60001-3434 GEOGRAPHICAL CODE=89-982300-0
THIS MULTI- FAMILY DWELLING ADDRESS WAS FIRST REPORTED 4/90 AND LAST REPORTED 5/93 BY UPDATE. LAST REPORTED BY CAR EXPO. ADDRESS REPORTED 3 TIMES.

                     1700 SOUTH BLVD
                     MOONTOWN MA 46533-1121 GEOGRAPHICAL CODE=84-782100-2
THIS MULTI- FAMILY DWELLING ADDRESS WAS FIRST REPORTED 7/88 AND LAST REPORTED 3/90 BY UPDATE. LAST REPORTED BY WINDY FIELDS. ADDRESS REPORTED 4 TIMES.

TELEPHONE #: (58)   847-436-0000 Residential
                     LAST REPORTED 3/96 BY BANCHOUSE
                     630-333-3333 Residential
                     LAST REPORTED 7/90 BY WINDY FIELDS

EMPLOYERS: (59)   WIDGET INC
                     ANYTOWN IL
REPORTED 4/95 BY INQUIRY. LAST REPORTED BY MASTER CAT.

                     SELF EMPLOYED
LAST REPORTED 5/89 BY INQUIRY. LAST REPORTED BY SUN FACTORY.

OTHER: (60)   DATE OF BIRTH: 11/05/1950
                     NAME: MARY A SMITH
                                        MARY A BROWN
                     HOME OWNERSHIP: Owns
                     SPOUSE NAME: N/A

ADDRESS REPORTED 2 TIMES. (61)
SOCIAL SECURITY NUMBER YOU GAVE WAS ISSUED: 1965 - 1969 (62)
ONFILE ADDRESS IDENTIFIED AS NON-RESIDENTIAL (63)

The "Identification Information" section follows the Please Help Us Help You section, and is the last section on the credit report. This section's function is to provide vital background information that has been supplied to the credit agency from the businesses that report information to them. The section has ten categories, which are listed and defined as follows:

Number	Abbreviation	Description
54	SOCIAL SECURITY NUMBER	Lists the social security number that has been reported to the credit agency from other organizations, along with the number of times the number has been reported. If other social security numbers have been used with your name, those numbers will appear along with the number of times they have been used.
55	DRIVER'S LICENSE NUMBER	Lists the driver's license number that has been reported to the credit agency for other organizations.
56	ADDRESSES	Lists all the addresses that have been used in relation to your credit habits—beginning from the most current address, going back to the earliest.
57	N/A	Lists residency information in coordination with the address category. Here, the report lists the type of residence for each address listed, who reported the information, and how many times the address was reported.
58	TELEPHONE NUMBER(S)	Lists all of the telephone numbers that have been reported to the credit agency from other organizations—beginning with most current.
59	EMPLOYERS	Lists all of the employers that have been reported to the credit agency from other organizations—beginning with the most current. The category also lists when the information was reported and who reported it.
60	OTHER	Lists four other vital pieces of background information that have been reported to the credit agency by other organizations. **Date of Birth:** Your date of birth. **Name:** All of the names you have used when filling out credit applications. **Home Ownership:** Whether you own a home or rent. **Spouse:** The name of your spouse, if applicable.
61	ADDRESS REPORTED	Lists the number of times your current address has been reported to the credit agency from other organizations.
62	SOCIAL SECURITY NUMBER ISSUED	Lists date when your social security number was issued.
63	ON-FILE ADDRESS	Lists whether your on-file address is reported as being residential or nonresidential.

Experian Sample Credit Report

Now that each section of the credit report has been broken down and explained, let's take a look at what the entire Experian credit report looks like with all of the sections in place. The information and numbering contained in this complete credit report is the same as in each of the individual sections discussed earlier.

This is your consumer identification number. Please refer to this number when you call or write.

ID# 1234561234   (1)

MARY A. SMITH
5000 MADE UP AVE.   (2)
ANYTOWN, IL 60006

HOW TO READ THIS REPORT: (3)

EXPERIAN IS THE INDEPENDENT COMPANY FORMED FROM TRW'S INFORMATION SERVICES BUSINESS.

AN EXPLANATORY ENCLOSURE ACCOMPANIES THIS REPORT. IT DESCRIBES YOUR CREDIT RIGHTS AND OTHER HELPFUL INFORMATION. IF THE ENCLOSURE IS MISSING, OR YOU HAVE QUESTIONS ABOUT THIS REPORT, PLEASE CONTACT THE OFFICE LISTED ON THE LAST PAGE.

AS PART OF OUR FRAUD-PREVENTION PROGRAM, ACCOUNT NUMBERS MAY NOT FULLY DISPLAY ON THIS REPORT.
          (4)

YOUR CREDIT HISTORY: (5)

THIS INFORMATION COMES FROM PUBLIC RECORDS OR ORGANIZATIONS THAT HAVE GRANTED CREDIT TO YOU. AN ASTERISK BY AN ACCOUNT INDICATES THAT THIS ITEM MAY REQUIRE FURTHER REVIEW BY A PROSPECTIVE CREDITOR WHEN CHECKING YOUR CREDIT HISTORY. IF YOU BELIEVE ANY OF THE INFORMATION IS INCORRECT, PLEASE LET US KNOW.

ACCOUNT	DESCRIPTION
(6)	(9) (10)
1 *US BKPT CT IL	VOLUNTARY BANKRUPTCY CHAPTER 7 DISCHARGED ON 01/10/90.
(7)	(11) (12) (13)
201 W WILSON STREET	PETITIONED ON 08/12/89. RECORDED ASSETS: $3,000, LIABILITIES: $54,200.
CHICAGO IL 60006	(14)
(8)	YOU ARE SOLELY RESPONSIBLE FOR THIS PUBLIC RECORD ITEM.
DOCKET #	
9231045	
	(15) (16) (17)
2 *SUING COUNTY COURT	SMALL CLAIMS CIVIL JUDGMENT SATISFIED ON 10/24/87. ORIGINAL FILING
PROFITS CNTY CT HOUSE	(18) (19) (14)
CHICAGO IL 60023	DATE 06/13/87. AMOUNT: $7000. PLAINTIFF: TOM AND JERRY. YOU ARE SOLELY
DOCKET #	RESPONSIBLE FOR THIS PUBLIC ITEM.
0001 ILM2700	
	(20) (21) (14)
3 *COOKED COUNTY FEDERAL	FEDERAL TAX LIEN ON 04/04/91. AMOUNT: $2500. YOU ARE SOLELY RESPONSIBLE FOR
COURT	THIS PUBLIC RECORD ITEM.
P O BOX 000	
CHICAGO IL 60606	
CERTIFICATE #	
91111400	

Experian Sample Credit Report — cont.

ACCOUNT	**DESCRIPTION**

(22)
4 *SMLA/LSCK
(23)
P O BOX 444
MISSING YOU IL 60607
(24)
BANKING
(25)
ACCT #
50008887XXXX

(26)   **(27)**   **(28)**
THIS EDUCATION LOAN WAS OPENED 10/20/91 AND HAS 120 MONTH REPAYMENT
(29)
TERMS. YOU HAVE CONTRACTUAL RESPONSIBILITY FOR THIS ACCOUNT AND ARE
(30)   **(31)**
PRIMARILY RESPONSIBLE FOR ITS PAYMENT. ORIGINAL AMOUNT: $2000.

(32)   **(33)**   **(34)**   **(35)**
AS OF 10/14/92, THIS ACCOUNT IS PAID. PREVIOUSLY WAS 90 DAYS PAST DUE. ORIGINAL DELINQUENCY
(36)
DATE 05/12/92. MONTHS REVIEWED: 12

5   VISA
P O BOX 700
BEDROCK IL 68880
BANKING
ACCT #
801100789111XXXX

THIS CREDIT CARD ACCOUNT WAS OPENED 04/09/87 AND HAS REVOLVING
REPAYMENT TERMS. YOU HAVE CONTRACTUAL RESPONSIBILITY FOR THIS ACCOUNT
AND PRIMARILY RESPONSIBLE FOR ITS PAYMENT. HIGH BALANCE: $3000

THIS CLOSED ACCOUNT IS 180 DAYS PAST DUE AND WAS 90 DAYS PAST DUE 2 OTHER TIME. SCHEDULED MONTHLY
PAYMENT: $50. LAST PAYMENT REPORTED TO EXPERIAN: 02/28/92. BALANCE: $3,000 ON 02/12/96. PAST DUE: $635.
MONTHS REVIEWED: 72.
(37)
PAYMENT HISTORY: 654321111111111111111- - - - - - -
(38)
TIMES LATE: 30=1, 60=0, 90+=2
** CREDIT LINE CLOSED - GRANTOR REQUEST - REPORTED BY SUBSCRIBER **
(39)
Balance History: Between 10-90 and 02-96 your credit limit was $3000. Between 04-87 and 03-89 your credit limit was $2800. Your balance
was:

6   GREAT AUTO BANK
757 BUMPER AVENUE
HEADLIGHT IL 60690
FINANCE
ACCT #
13215250003XXXX

THIS AUTOLOAN WAS OPENED 06/16/94 AND HAS 60 MONTH REPAYMENT TERMS.
YOU HAVE CONTRACTUAL RESPONSIBILITY FOR THIS ACCOUNT AND ARE PRIMARILY
RESPONSIBLE FOR ITS PAYMENT. ORIGINAL AMOUNT: $22,000.

AS OF 05/12/95, THIS OPEN ACCOUNT IS CURRENT AND ALL PAYMENTS ARE BEING MADE ON TIME. SCHEDULED
MONTHLY PAYMENT: $325. LAST PAYMENT REPORTED TO EXPERIAN: 05/08/96. BALANCE $19,450 ON 05/15/96. MONTHS
REVIEWED: 24.
(39)
Balance History: The original amount of this account was $22,000. Your balance was:

04/15/96 - $19600,	03/15/96 - $19750,	02/15/96 - $19900,	01/15/96 - $20050,
12/15/96 - $20200,	11/15/95 - $20350,	10/15/95 - $20500,	09/15/95 - $20650,
08/08/96 - $20800,	07/07/95 - $20950,	06/07/95 - $21100,	05/07/95 - $21250,
04/07/95 - $21400,	03/07/95 - $21550,	02/07/95 - $21700,	01/08/95 - $21850,
12/15/94 - $22000.			

Experian Sample Credit Report — cont.

ACCOUNT	DESCRIPTION
7 BANCHOUSE 800 JORDAN'S WAY CHICAGO IL 01102 FINANCE ACCT # 913642XXXX	THIS CONVENTIONAL REAL ESTATE MORTGAGE WAS OPENED 12/03/92 AND HAS 30 YEAR REPAYMENT TERMS. YOU HAVE CONTRACTUAL RESPONSIBILITY FOR THIS ACCOUNT AND ARE PRIMARILY RESPONSIBLE FOR ITS REPAYMENT. ORIGINAL AMOUNT: $78,000.

AS OF 01/15/96, THIS OPEN ACCOUNT IS CURRENT AND ALL PAYMENTS ARE BEING MADE ON TIME. SCHEDULED MONTHLY PAYMENT: $725. LAST PAYMENT REPORTED TO EXPERIAN: 05/15/96. BALANCE $64,000 ON 05/15/96. MONTHS REVIEWED: 31.

Balance History: The original amount of this account was $78,000. Your balance was:

04/15/96 - $64200,	03/15/96 - $64400,	02/15/96 - $64600,	01/15/96 - $64800,
12/15/96 - $65000,	11/15/95 - $65200,	10/15/95 - $65400,	09/15/95 - $65600,
08/08/96 - $65800,	07/07/95 - $66000,	06/07/95 - $66200,	05/07/95 - $66400,
04/07/95 - $66600,	03/07/95 - $66800,	02/07/95 - $67000,	01/08/95 - $67200,
12/15/94 - $67400,	11/15/94 - $67600,	10/15/94 - $67800,	09/15/94 - $68000.

YOUR CREDIT HISTORY WAS REVIEWED BY:

THE FOLLOWING INQUIRIES ARE REPORTED TO THOSE WHO ASK TO REVIEW YOUR CREDIT HISTORY.

INQUIRY	DESCRIPTION
(41)	(44) (45)
8 CAR EXPO CENTER (42) 123 WEST CEDAR THE TOWN IL 60670 (43) FINANCE	03 / 11 / 96 INQUIRY MADE FOR EXTENSION OF CREDIT, REVIEW OR OTHER PERMISSIBLE PURPOSE.
9 NPC / FST P O BOX 4500 WISHINGTON DC 88809 BANKING	05 / 31 / 95 INQUIRY MADE FOR EXTENSION OF CREDIT, REVIEW OR OTHER PERMISSIBLE PURPOSE.
10 LPC / HTC 101 CLEAVER STREET BUTCHER IL 60606 FINANCE	05 / 31 / 95 INQUIRY MADE FOR EXTENSION OF CREDIT, REVIEW OR OTHER PERMISSIBLE PURPOSE.
11 SEARS ROEBUCK & CO. 1000 SOUTH AVENUE ESTATES HOFFMAN IL 60607 FINANCE	08 / 07 / 95 INQUIRY MADE FOR EXTENSION OF CREDIT, REVIEW OR OTHER PERMISSIBLE PURPOSE.

THE FOLLOWING INQUIRIES ARE NOT REPORTED TO THOSE WHO ASK TO REVIEW YOUR CREDIT HISTORY. THEY ARE INCLUDED SO THAT YOU HAVE A COMPLETE LIST OF INQUIRIES. (46)

	INQUIRY	DESCRIPTION
12	CREDIT CHECK P O BOX 1234 SIMPLE TOWN WI 48756 NATL CREDIT CARDS	09 / 12 / 95 INQUIRY MADE FOR PRESCREEN PROGRAM. YOUR FILE WAS MATCHED AGAINST THIS CREDITOR'S CRITERIA TO DEVELOP A LIST OF NAMES FOR A CREDIT OFFER OR SERVICE.
13	MASTER CARD 23 GRAND CANYON DRIVE BIG HOLE OH 34567 NATL CREDIT CARDS	02 / 02 / 94 INQUIRY MADE FOR PRESCREEN PROGRAM. YOUR FILE WAS MATCHED AGAINST THIS CREDITOR'S CRITERIA TO DEVELOP A LIST OF NAMES FOR A CREDIT OFFER OR SERVICE.
14	GREAT AUTO BANK 765 CHESTER AVENUE FRONT SEAT IL 60697 FINANCE	04 / 10 / 94 INQUIRY MADE FOR PURPOSES OF ACCOUNT REVIEW.
15	JEWEL FOOD SERVICES 1000 LETTUCE STREET FROZEN IL 60687	04 / 11 / 94 INQUIRY MADE FOR PURPOSES OF ACCOUNT REVIEW.

PLEASE HELP US HELP YOU: (47)

AT EXPERIAN WE KNOW HOW IMPORTANT YOUR GOOD CREDIT IS TO YOU. IT IS EQUALLY IMPORTANT TO US THAT OUR INFORMATION BE ACCURATE AND UP TO DATE. LISTED BELOW IS THE INFORMATION YOU GAVE US WHEN YOU ASKED FOR THIS REPORT. IF THE INFORMATION IS NOT CORRECT OR YOU DID NOT SUPPLY US WITH YOUR FULL NAME, ADDRESS FOR THE PAST 5 YEARS, SOCIAL SECURITY NUMBER AND YEAR OF BIRTH; THIS REPORT MAY NOT BE COMPLETE. IF THIS INFORMATION IS INCOMPLETE OR NOT ACCURATE, PLEASE LET US KNOW.

YOUR NAME: (48)   MARY A SMITH

SOCIAL SECURITY #: (51) 000-00-0000
DATE OF BIRTH: (52) 11 / 05 / 1950

ADDRESS: (49)   5000 MADE UP AVE
ANYTOWN IL 60006

SPOUSE: (53) N/A

OTHER ADDRESSES: (50)   1000 MAIN STREET
WALKING IL 60001

IDENTIFICATION INFORMATION:

THE FOLLOWING ADDITIONAL INFORMATION HAS BEEN PROVIDED TO US BY ORGANIZATIONS THAT REPORT INFORMATION TO US.

SOCIAL SECURITY #:   000-00-0000 REPORTED 10 TIMES.
(54)

DRIVERS LICENSE #:   IL 60050050577
(55)   LAST REPORTED 3 / 96

ADDRESSES: (56)   5000 MADE UP AVENUE
                     ANYTOWN IL 60006-7869 GEOGRAPHICAL CODE=78-987600-7

(57)
THIS SINGLE FAMILY DWELLING ADDRESS WAS FIRST REPORTED 6 / 93 AND LAST REPORTED 3/96 BY UPDATE. LAST REPORTED BY BANCHOUSE. ADDRESS REPORTED 7 TIMES.

                     1000 MAIN STREET
                     WALKING IL 60001-3434 GEOGRAPHICAL CODE=89-982300-0

THIS MULTI- FAMILY DWELLING ADDRESS WAS FIRST REPORTED 4 / 90 AND LAST REPORTED 5/93 BY UPDATE. LAST REPORTED BY CAR EXPO. ADDRESS REPORTED 3 TIMES.

                     1700 SOUTH BLVD
                     MOONTOWN MA 46533-1121 GEOGRAPHICAL CODE=84-782100-2

THIS MULTI- FAMILY DWELLING ADDRESS WAS FIRST REPORTED 7 / 88 AND LAST REPORTED 3/90 BY UPDATE. LAST REPORTED BY WINDY FIELDS. ADDRESS REPORTED 4 TIMES.

TELEPHONE #: (58)   847-436-0000 Residential
                     LAST REPORTED 3/96 BY BANCHOUSE
                     630-333-3333 Residential
                     LAST REPORTED 7/90 BY WINDY FIELDS

EMPLOYERS: (59)   WIDGET INC
                     ANYTOWN IL
REPORTED 4/95 BY INQUIRY. LAST REPORTED BY MASTER CAT.

                     SELF EMPLOYED
LAST REPORTED 5/89 BY INQUIRY. LAST REPORTED BY SUN FACTORY.

OTHER: (60)   DATE OF BIRTH: 11/ 05 / 1950
                     NAME: MARY A SMITH
                                       MARY A BROWN
                     HOME OWNERSHIP: Owns
                     SPOUSE NAME: N/A

ADDRESS REPORTED 2 TIMES. (61)
SOCIAL SECURITY NUMBER YOU GAVE WAS ISSUED: 1965 - 1969 (62)
ONFILE ADDRESS IDENTIFIED AS NON-RESIDENTIAL (63)

Chapter 6

You've Got Your Credit Report

If you don't think your credit report plays a significant role when dealing with lenders, think again. Your credit rating has a direct correlation to your ability to acquire a loan. Today more than ever, lenders score your credit based on a number of predetermined factors. The number one factor is being able to show your ability to be a responsible credit consumer. Lenders take this information directly from your credit report, no ifs, ands, or buts.

Ordering a copy of your credit report is easy; however, knowing what lenders and other creditors are looking for is not. Almost every piece of information on your credit report is used one way or another by lenders when making a decision about your credit worthiness. Lenders also figure in other outside factors when determining credit worthiness. So, it is important to understand what is important to lenders.

WHAT ARE LENDERS LOOKING FOR?

Lenders let you use their money in order to make money. The more people use their money to purchase items, the more money comes back to them in interest, resulting in profit for the lender. However, in order to have the privilege of using a lender's money, a lender must first determine who will pay them back and who will not pay them back. Each lender uses their own formula for determining who will be considered and who will not be considered.

I am sure you have gone through, or will go through, the process of applying for credit. The credit application process can be a trying experience, especially if you are unaware of your current credit status. First you fill out the credit application. Some credit applications just ask for the basic background information, such as name, address, phone, employment, and income. On the other hand, some credit applications delve deeply into your personal and consumer information and ask for bank names, checking and savings account numbers, friends' names and contact information, and the type of car you own. After you fill out the credit application, you return it to the lender and wait for a reply. Not too long ago, waiting up to a week before hearing whether your application was approved or rejected was considered acceptable, but not today. Today's technology allows most lenders instant access to the information needed to make a qualified decision within a day.

TYPES OF LENDERS

If one lender tells you "no," there is always another who will tell you "yes." As stated earlier, every lender uses a different formula for determining who will be accepted and who will be turned away. At one end of the spectrum are "primary lenders," lenders who are very conservative in their lending practices, taking very little risk. Most primary lenders are not willing to take a chance on you if there is any indication of credit risk. The primary lenders usually have the best reputation for reliability, along with the lowest interest rates. Most primary lenders do not ask for all of your detailed information on a credit application.

In the middle of the spectrum are "sub-primary lenders," lenders who are more liberal in their lending practices, taking some risk. Most sub-primary lenders are usually reliable and have interest rates that are slightly higher than the primary lenders'. When filling out credit applications for a sub-primary lending institution, you will find a good mix of those who want all of your information and those who don't.

At the other end of the spectrum are "secondary lenders," lenders who will accept just about anyone, regardless of credit. Secondary lenders specialize in giving people with credit problems the opportunity to get credit and begin rebuilding their credit. However, there is a price to pay—secondary lenders usually have very high interest rates. Secondary lenders know they are many people's last hope for credit, so they are able to charge higher than average interest rates. Also with the need for credit as important as it is in society today, there are thousands of secondary lenders throughout the United States. Reliability is a very important concern when using a secondary lender. Before choosing a secondary lender, do some research first to find out their track record. You can research the lender by contacting your local branch of the Better Business Bureau (page 87) or other similar organizations. Since secondary lenders take the greatest chance of losing money, they ask for the greatest amount of information when filling out a credit application. Secondary lenders will ask for all of the information you would give to a primary lender and sub-primary lender, plus items such as references, proof of address (e.g., utility bill), a copy of your driver's license, proof of paid charge-offs, and proof of income.

WHAT IS CREDIT ANALYSIS?

Regardless of whether you are dealing with a primary lender, sub-primary lender, or a secondary lender, all three look at specific areas when making a credit worthiness decision. An individual's credit worthiness is determined through a process called a "credit analysis." Lenders put together a credit analysis from the information the consumer reporting agencies gather, along with other outside factors. Lenders focus on at least one of the following areas when making a credit worthiness decision:

	Area Looked At	Information Found In
1	Credit Standing	Credit Report
2	Credit Capacity	Credit Report and Income
3	Character	Outside References
4	General Reputation	Credit Report and Outside References
5	Mode of Living	Credit Report/Income/Assets
6	Collateral	Available Assets
7	Human Factor(s)	Life Experiences

One of the outside factors that plays a role in determining credit worthiness is "The Human Factor." This a useful tool when dealing with sub-primary and secondary lenders.

The Human Factor

In theory, credit worthiness should be based strictly on the indicators that show an individual's credit strengths and weaknesses. However, not all decisions are so cut-and-dried, due to what I call the "human factor." Every time a credit analysis is compiled, a human being must review the information. The human factor is based on the assumption that we are all human beings and that all human beings make mistakes. The human factor relies upon the fact that everyone makes mistakes, but that doesn't necessarily make someone a bad person. In all likelihood the person who is analyzing your credit worthiness has had credit problems of their own, making them more sympathetic to your situation. The closer you can bring someone to your situation, the better your chance that person will help you. The human factor reinforces the importance of getting to know the person(s) you are dealing with and being completely honest with them.

The All-in-One Lending Institution

Some larger lending institutions are arranged into primary, sub-primary and secondary departments, attempting to capture a greater segment of the consumer credit market. The larger institutions that are arranged in this manner present the greatest opportunity. If you apply for credit with one of these lenders, depending on the lender's interpretation of your credit worthiness, you can be placed into one of the three departments. Usually, regardless of what department you go through, your credit report will show you have an account with the larger institution, benefiting you in the long run. However, do not take that for granted. Ask the lender if they report to a credit agency as a regular account, as opposed to a secondary account.

One other possible benefit of using a lender who provides all three segments is loyalty. Even if your first loan was at a higher interest due to some credit difficulties, you can use that lender again. If you show the lender your ability to keep up with your responsibilities, the next time you use that lender, you may get a much lower interest rate.

Chapter 7

Let's Start Cleaning Up Your Credit Report

Okay, now that you have a copy of your credit report and you know what lenders are looking for, you can begin to go through your report and determine what areas need to be fixed. This is extremely important. The key to successfully strengthening your credit situation depends on your thoroughness and accuracy.

You must start at the beginning of your report, going over each section carefully. When checking each section, take your time; the more accurate you are, the higher your success rate. To assist you in your efforts, we have created an easy-to-follow process. Follow each step and complete any and all inserts or worksheets. The process is divided into four stages:

The Four Stages

Stage 1   Determine the trouble spots

Stage 2   Make a list ("note pad" inserts)

Stage 3   Take action

Stage 4   Revise your goals

STAGE 1: DETERMINE THE TROUBLE SPOTS

When determining the trouble spots on your credit report every detail is important, so take your time and look at everything. Begin by checking spellings, first name, last name, middle initial, date of birth, abbreviations, current and previous addresses and employers, social security number, etc. A lender can decide not to accept your application for credit if the information in this section is incorrect, there are inconsistencies with your application, or if the information is not up to date. After carefully looking over all of the information, you should highlight the information you feel to be incorrect or inaccurate.

Check all of the public record information, making sure the records posted to your credit report belong to you. If you have records in this section, take a closer look at them, making sure they are listed correctly. Pay close attention to whether the account number is reported correctly, the court and dates are correct, the liabilities and assets are accurate, the type of public record is correct, the record is reported as paid or unpaid, and the docket number and parties involved are listed accurately. You want to highlight on the credit report any inconsistencies between what you believe to be correct and what the credit report is saying.

Check all of the account information, making sure the accounts posted to your report belong to you. Check the accuracy of the account names, the date accounts were opened, high credits, the date the last time the accounts were reported, account balances, payment patterns, the MOPs, account numbers, terms, the date accounts were closed, the number of signers on the account, and the account description. Highlight the information you feel is inaccurate or incorrect.

The most important area to look at is the payment history area. The payment history area lists the month-to-month payment histories of each account. Having the payment history section correct and up to date is a vital part of maintaining strong credit. Creditors want to see that you can pay your monthly responsibilities on time; therefore, creditors place a lot of importance on the payment history area. Inaccurate and incorrect information can lead to credit denial. If you believe that your report reflects inaccurate or incorrect information, highlight the information. Be sure that you have documentation that will support your claims.

Check all of the inquiry information, making sure that all of the names listed under this section are familiar to you. In order for a lender to pull your credit report, they must first have your permission, accompanied by your signature. Only you can give someone permission to check your credit. If any of the names listed under this section are unfamiliar to you, highlight them on the credit report. The fewer inquiries you have listed on your credit report, the stronger your credit rating.

Finally, if applicable, check the consumer statement information. Similar to the inquiry section, you are the only one who can add a consumer statement to your credit report. If you have never requested a consumer statement be added to your report, there should not be one. Once again, note any discrepancies by highlighting the information you feel to be inaccurate or incorrect.

STAGE 2: CORRECT MISTAKES USING THE "NOTE PADS"

Once you have gone through and highlighted all of the incorrect or questionable information, you are going to transfer the information to the appropriate "Note Pad" insert.

What Is a "Note Pad"?

The Note Pads are inserts that allow you to better organize the inaccurate or incorrect information that you highlighted on your credit report. The Note Pads are found in Appendix E. Each credit report has its own set of Note Pads that coincide with its section.

Under each of the sections, the relevant categories are listed along with the number where you can find that specific category on the credit report. Because you have no control over certain categories of your credit report, such as codes assigned by the credit agencies, some of the categories have been left out.

How to Use the Note Pads

When you begin filling in the Note Pads, start by providing the identification information such as name, social security number, date of birth, name of account, docket number, or account number. Be sure you fill this information in each time you start a new Note Pad. After you provide the necessary identification information, you can move on to the individual categories.

The categories are listed, as closely as possible, in the order in which they appear on the credit report, under the heading "Credit Report Category." The next heading is "Status." In the status column you will indicate either "Okay" or "Review."

The next two columns should only be completed if you placed a "Review" in the previous column. After the "Status" column, you will see the "Reason" column. If you feel a category should be reviewed, explain your reasoning. Be specific when explaining why you feel the category is incorrect or inaccurate. The last column, "Replace with the Following Information," allows you to enter the correct information for the category in question.

All of the Note Pad inserts, except for Insert KK, which is used for the Equifax credit report, have the same four columns.

Since you will be using the information from the inserts to fill out other inserts, accuracy and neatness are important. Be sure to use a different Note Pad for each public record, account, and inquiry you question.

Note Pad Letter	Description
AA	General Information
BB	Summary Line Information
CC	Public Record Information
DD	Account Information
EE	Inquiry Information
FF	Consumer Statement Information
GG	Personal Identification Information
HH	Public Record Information
II	Collection Account Information
JJ	Credit Account Information
KK	Additional Information
LL	Companies That Requested Your Credit File
MM	Your Credit History (Public Records) Information
NN	Your Credit History (Account History) Information
OO	Your Credit History Was Reviewed By Information
PP	Please Help Us Help You Information
QQ	Identification Information

STAGE 3: PREPARE TO TAKE ACTION

Now that you have completed the appropriate Note Pad inserts, listing the area(s) you feel need to be corrected or investigated, you are ready to begin. Your first course of action will be sending the prepared letters to the credit agencies and organizations with which you are having trouble.

However, before you begin sending out letters, you should know a little bit about the laws and regulations that help to protect you. The Fair Credit Reporting Act (FCRA) is a law that helps to protect your rights as a credit-using consumer.

What Is the Fair Credit Reporting Act?

The Fair Credit Reporting Act is a federal statute that was put into effect to monitor consumer reporting agencies, individuals who use consumer reporting agencies, and consumer concerns about information on credit reports and the information contained in credit files.

What Is the FCRA's Purpose?

The purpose of the FCRA is "to require that consumer reporting agencies adopt reasonable procedures for the meeting of commerce for consumer credit, personnel, insurance, and other information in a manner which is fair and equitable to the consumer, with regard to the confidentiality, accuracy, relevancy, and proper utilization of such information."

The law is designed to make sure information that is inaccurate, incorrect, or misleading does not stay on an individual's credit report. Also under the FCRA, credit agencies must have procedures set up for gathering, maintaining, and passing along information in a timely manner. The adherence to these procedures is enforced by the Federal Trade Commission. Information regarding the Federal Trade Commission is discussed in greater detail later in the book.

What Can a Credit Agency Put on Your Credit Report?

Credit agencies have a broad spectrum from which to choose when putting information into your credit file and onto your credit report. A credit agency can collect and report information in regard to your: credit worthiness, credit standing, credit limits, character, reputation, and personal characteristics. Credit agencies also have the right to gather and report all criminal activities, public records, collection accounts, bankruptcies, and paid or unpaid tax liens.

To Whom Can the Credit Agencies Give Your Credit Information?

A credit agency may release your credit report information in any of the following situations:

1. A credit transaction for legitimate business purposes.
2. A review of a collection account.
3. An application for a government license.
4. A government agency determining benefits by checking financial status.
5. A future employer or current employer for hiring and promoting purposes.
6. An application for insurance.
7. A court order or federal grand jury subpoena.
8. A signed request by you.
9. An FBI investigation.

How Long Can a Credit Agency Report Unfavorable Information to My Credit Report?

According to the FCRA, a credit agency can report unfavorable information such as Chapter 13 bankruptcies, collection accounts, late payments, judgments, and even repossessions, up to seven years after the information is first reported as unfavorable. However, there are exceptions to this rule. Some bankruptcy information such as: Chapter 7, Chapter 11, and Chapter 12 can be reported up to ten years from the original filing date. As a side note, inquiries remain on your credit report anywhere from six months to two years depending on the source of the inquiry.

To Find Out More about the FCRA

Additional information regarding the FCRA can be found in the government section at your local library, law library, or school library. The information will be located in the government documents section. You can also contact your local chapter of the FTC or Better Business Bureau and ask them if they can provide you with any additional information.

STAGE 4: REVISE YOUR ORIGINAL GOALS

Now that you have taken a more in-depth look at your credit situation, you should revise your goals. As was the case for the first goals, your revised goals should be reachable, measurable, and time sensitive. However, unlike your first goals, the revised goals should be very specific regarding what you are trying to obtain. Breaking down your credit problem into obtainable goals greatly increases your chances for success. Let's first take a look at some examples of goals that are specific, reachable, measurable, and time sensitive; then using Insert C, rewrite your goals.

Revised Goals:

1. I, (Your Name), want to strengthen my credit report by adding (Account Name) to my credit report by (date).

2. I, (Your Name), want to correct my credit report by replacing an incorrect home address with my correct home address by (date).

3. I, (Your Name), want to strengthen my credit report by deleting (Inquiry Name) from my credit report by (date).

## Chapter 8

Strengthening Your Credit Report

In order to start strengthening your credit rating, you have to make some changes. Making changes in your lifestyle and spending habits are important and helpful areas to focus on when strengthening your credit rating. However, actually changing the information on your credit report can be just as important and helpful.

We have already gone over what you can do to prevent bad credit from happening and how you can establish and re-establish your credit. Now let's take a look at what you can do to change the appearance of your credit report. Depending on the severity of credit trouble, changing the appearance of your credit report can be done by using one or all of the following methods listed below.

Change the Appearance of Your Credit Report By:

A   Updating your credit report and file.

B   Adding new accounts to your credit report.

C   Deleting accounts from your credit report.

D   Changing delinquent payments into good payments.

E   Knowing where to send your letters.

UPDATING YOUR CREDIT REPORT AND CREDIT FILE

Updating your credit report and credit file is an important part of maintaining a good credit rating. Because a lender can base a credit worthiness decision on discrepancies between the information you provide on a credit application and the information on your credit report, you must keep your credit information up to date. For instance, have you recently experienced any of the following life changes?

Have You Recently:

Changed your name (first, last, middle, spelling)

Changed your marital status (divorced, married, separated)

Changed your place of residency

Changed your place of employment

Changed your social security number

Changed the status of an account (open, closed, number of signers)

Changed the status of a bankruptcy (type, discharge, reaffirmation)

Requested information be changed on your credit report

Any time you have a life change such as the ones listed, you should have your credit report updated as soon as possible. In time, your credit report may update itself; however, you do not want to wait that long. While you just sit back and wait, the agencies could be placing incorrect or inaccurate information into your credit file and onto your credit report.

You should contact the credit agency immediately after going through a life change. The sooner you report the change to the credit agencies, the more likely your credit information will be accurate and up to date. Credit agencies welcome your thoroughness.

When sending updated account information to the credit agencies, use Letter #10 from Appendix A, along with Insert D when writing to Trans-Union, Insert E when writing to Equifax, or Insert F when writing to Experian (Appendix D).

Adding New Accounts to Your Credit Report

Depending upon a number of variables, some businesses do not report to credit agencies; therefore, your credit information does not show up on a credit report.

One of the reasons you use credit is to build up your credit file and to strengthen your credit rating. Your credit worthiness should not be jeopardized due to the fact that some businesses choose not to report their information to a credit agency. In accordance with the Fair Credit Reporting Act, credit agencies have a responsibility to provide complete and accurate consumer credit information.

The first step you can take in strengthening your credit situation is to write to the credit agencies and request that they add your good accounts if they do not appear on your credit report. Since the main purpose behind adding accounts to your credit report is to strengthen your report, you only want to add accounts that are deemed to be good, up-to-date accounts.

When deciding which accounts you are going to add to your report, you should choose the accounts that have had the highest original balance, longest payment history, or were most recently paid in full.

In order to ensure the credit agencies correctly use the information you send, you must follow a few guidelines.

First, be specific as to what action you would like the credit agency to take. The letter and insert you will send will allow you to be specific. Be sure to use a separate insert for each account you are attempting to add.

Second, go to or write the business whose account you are adding to your credit report. Ask them for some kind of official record showing your payment pattern. A computer-generated printout would be the best; however, if the business does not use a computer, a hand-written, signed document should be sufficient.

Third, make copies of all billing statements, cancelled checks, and payment information. Send copies of all documentation proving the account to be added is legitimate. Never send the original copies of any documentation. The originals are your proof of the account.

Finally, use Letter #11 from Appendix A and Insert G from Appendix D when writing to the credit agency.

CHANGING DELINQUENT PAYMENTS TO GOOD PAYMENTS

In order to maintain a good credit rating, you must constantly be aware of your credit situation. Any one of life's unforeseen misfortunes can lead to the neglecting of your credit responsibilities. Late payments or missing payments on accounts can destroy your credit worthiness. If your credit already reflects late or missed payments, you want to try and have those delinquent payments changed into good payments.

The only way you will be able to change your accounts is by contacting the lender and coming up with a reasonable plan of action that will benefit both parties. For example, if you know in advance you are going to have trouble paying a bill, contact the lender immediately. By contacting the lender ahead of time you set up an open line of communication between you and the lender and it is more likely your credit will stay intact.

Many situations can arise where it would be advantageous for you to contact the lender. Here are a few reasons to contact the lender:

Contact the Lender When . . .

1 You make a late payment (one time)
2 You can't make the monthly payment (short term/long term)
3 Your account is turned over to a collection agency

You Make a Late Payment (One Time)

No human being is perfect one hundred percent of the time. The "human factor," which was discussed earlier, is based on the premise that mistakes are made by everybody including you, me, and even the lenders.

A late payment is not the end of the world or your good credit. However, if you do make a late payment, contacting the lender with a letter of apology can help strengthen your relationship with that lender. Assure the lender that your late payment is a one-time incident due to a miscommunication on your part. Reinforce the importance of having good credit, and emphasizing your loyalty. Also in your letter of apology, you can ask the lender not to report the account as late. Having the lender report your account as on time and up to date should be your main objective.

If, however, the account has already been reported as being late, you need to get the company's help in changing the account. If at all possible, you should deal with one person. The fewer people involved in the process, the less room for confusion.

Once an agreement is made, you want to try and get something in writing from the lender. Any agreements made should always be in writing. A verbal commitment is okay; however, have the lender send you written documentation after the fact.

When attempting to contact and set up an arrangement with the company, use Letter #12 from the Appendix A and Insert H from Appendix D.

Letter #12 explains why your payment was late, and that it was a one-time error. Insert H is sent to the company. A company representative should fill out and sign this insert, stating your account was reported to the agency in error.

As soon as you receive the written verification back from the company, send Letter #13 and a copy of Insert H to the credit agency. Insert H should have been sent back to you from the company, with a company representative's signature. Letter #13 asks the credit agency to reinvestigate the account.

You Can't Make the Monthly Payment (short term/long term)

If you have an account on which you are unable to make monthly payments, due to any circumstances, contact the lender. As long as the account information has not been turned over to a collection agency, your credit worthiness can still be salvaged.

Take a look at the following table. Are any of the reasons surrounding your inability to meet your monthly credit responsibilities listed below?

Reasons You May Be Unable to Make Payments:
1 Divorce
2 Loss of Employment
3 Illness
4 Financial Difficulties
5 Legal Trouble
6 Natural Disaster (flood, tornado, earthquake, etc.)

Whatever your reasons are for not being able to pay, you still have an important bargaining tool on your side. A lender will be more willing to work with you in order to avoid turning the account over to a collection agency and losing money.

After a lender exhausts all attempts at retrieving the money that is owed on an account, the lender usually writes the account off as a "bad debt." After the account is put into the bad debt file, the lender usually turns the account over to a collection agency. Lenders hire collection agencies to help retrieve accounts that are considered to be bad debts. Once an account is turned over to a collection agency, the responsibility of retrieving the money rests on the shoulders of the collection agency. If the agency is able to retrieve the money owed on the account, they receive a percentage of the amount collected.

Some larger organizations have their own in-house collection agencies. Regardless of whether an organization has their own in-house agency or has to hire an outside agency, a collection department is still an added expense.

If you were or are unable to make your monthly payments due to any of the situations detailed earlier in the table or any other legitimate reason, you need to formulate a plan. In order to execute your plan, you need to immediately contact the lender with whom you are having the trouble. The sooner you are able to contact the lender, the better your chances of saving your credit rating. Initial contact of the lender can be done by using Letter #14 from Appendix A and Inserts I and H from Appendix D. Letter #14 initiates the setting up of a payment plan between you and the lender. Insert I lists the details of the payment plan. Insert H is also sent to the company. A company representative should fill out and sign this insert, stating your account was reported to the agency in error.

As soon as you receive the information back from the company, send Letter #13 from Appendix A and a copy of Insert H to the credit agency. Insert H should have been sent back to you from the company, with a company representative's signature. Letter #13 asks the credit agency to reinvestigate the account.

Your Account Is Turned Over to a Collection Agency

Let's say, for one reason or another, you were unable to contact the lender ahead of time to let them know you could not make the monthly payments. And because you could not contact the lender, your account was turned over to a collection agency. All hope of salvaging your credit is still not lost; but your chances of success are greatly reduced.

At this point, the only way you can hope to get your situation turned around is with good, hard, solid evidence. You must provide the lender with solid information as to why you were unable to make the monthly payments and why you did not contact them during this time period.

Your reason should be similar to the ones in the previous table, backed with supportive documentation. Along with the documentation supporting your case, include a payment plan. The payment plan will show the lender that you have good intentions and are sincere about resolving the situation.

If your account has been turned over to a collection agency, and your best excuse is that the dog buried the phone bill in the backyard, don't even try.

When contacting the lender use Letter #15 from Appendix A and Inserts I and H from Appendix D. Letter #15 details the reasons why you were or are unable to make your monthly payments and suggests a payment plan be initiated. Insert I lists the details of the payment plan. Insert H asks the credit agencies to change your credit report, due to a reporting error.

As soon as you receive the information back from the company, send Letter #13 and a copy of Insert H, which has been returned from the company with a company representative's signature, to the credit agency, asking them to investigate the account.

DELETING ACCOUNTS FROM YOUR CREDIT REPORT

The following table lists several reasons why you would want to have an account removed from your credit report. Credit agencies actually encourage you to dispute any information that you consider incorrect. Because agencies are judged according to the accuracy of their information, agencies depend on you to keep them abreast of any problems associated with your credit report. Removing one or all of the following accounts from your credit report can be extremely beneficial to your credit worthiness.

Accounts to Be Removed from Your Credit Report
1   This Account Does Not Belong to Me
2   This Is an Outdated Account
3   This Account No Longer Exists

This Account Doesn't Belong to Me

Sometimes information gets mixed up either when it's getting reported to the credit agency, or to the credit report. If, for example, you are a Junior and your father is a Senior, your information could get mixed up due to the similarities in names. Having a similar social security number to someone else is another example of how information could get mixed up. Whatever the case may be, accounts not belonging to you should be removed from your credit report.

Removing a negative account that is not yours is self-explanatory. You do not want someone else's information jeopardizing your good credit even if the wrong account information is being reported as a good account. Most lenders look at the balance of all accounts, including accounts that haven't been used for a long time. Any additional accounts will damage your Debt-to-Income Ratio, putting a strain on your credit worthiness.

When attempting to have an account removed, you will be dealing directly with a credit agency. Because credit agencies are responsible for placing information on your credit report, let them handle the necessary research. All you have to do is provide the necessary information to help expedite the process.

If you have not contacted a company representative, but you know the account does not belong to you, send Letter #16 from Appendix A and Insert N from Appendix D. Letter #16 informs the credit agencies that the account information you have specified does not belong to you. Insert N lists the details of the account that you would like removed.

If you are in contact with someone from the company who can verify that you do not have an account with them, send Letter #13 and a copy of Insert H to the credit agency. Letter #13 allows you to pass along the name of the person who will verify that the account in question is not yours. Insert H, which should have been sent to the person you are in contact with at the company, allows you to send written verification that the account in question is not yours. The contact should have signed the Insert H and sent it back to you.

This Is an Outdated Account

As stated earlier, according to the FCRA credit agencies are allowed to keep old account information on your credit report anywhere from seven to ten years, depending on the type of account. Inquiries can remain on your credit report anywhere from six months to two years. Making sure old accounts and inquiries are removed from your credit report can be extremely beneficial to your credit worthiness. However, you should not remove old accounts that are yours and are deemed good. Past positive credit experience helps build your credit stability.

If you have a negative account, other than a bankruptcy, on your credit report that is older than seven years, you can have that account information removed. As stated earlier, most bankruptcies are allowed to be reported up to 10 years, with exception of a Chapter 13 bankruptcy. After 10 years, you can have the account information removed from your credit report.

Initiating the removal of an old account from your credit report requires that you write to the credit agency. The credit agency will perform its own investigation by contacting the appropriate source of the account in question. If the source the credit agency contacts does not respond, the credit agency must remove the old account from your credit file and credit report. Any documentation you might have proving your case should be sent along with the sample letter(s) and insert(s).

You can also perform the procedure in the above paragraphs with accounts that are not older than the required time allowed by credit agencies. After a reasonable amount of time, you can request that the credit agency reinvestigate your account. Sometimes if the account is old enough, you have a good chance of the business not responding back due to such factors as going out of business or not wanting to spend the time and money to respond.

The removal of old inquiries is handled in the same manner. If you have inquiries on your credit report that are over two years old, have them removed.

Also, if you have a consumer statement detailing a past credit problem on your credit report, and have since had the credit information deleted, you need to remove the consumer statement. There is no need to have a consumer statement on your credit report detailing a credit problem that does not exist.

When writing to the credit agencies use Letter #17 in Appendix A and Insert K in Appendix D to remove account information. Use Letter #18 and Insert L to remove inquiry information, and use Letter #19 and Insert M to remove a consumer statement.

I'll Pay My Account in Full, If the Account No Longer Exists

Another way you can have an account deleted from your credit report is by contacting the organization to which you owe money and setting up an agreement. Most companies will do everything within their power to collect money owed. Using the money owed a company as a bargaining tool will help you achieve your goal.

You will begin by sending a letter to the organization you owe money, informing them of your intention to remove negative information from your credit report. Furthermore, in return for their help in removing the negative information from your credit report, you will pay your account with them in full.

In order to successfully complete this task, you need to deal with a specific person from the organization. The person must have the authority within the organization to help you. Your goal is to get the company representative to report your account as unverifiable in return for full payment of your account.

Before proceeding, you must have a contact within the organization and a written, signed agreement from the organization, stating their intentions. Once you have those two items, you can proceed to the next part. When contacting the company use Letter #20 from Appendix A and Insert J from Appendix D.

The second half of this plan involves the credit agency. Once you have a written and signed agreement from the organization stating the account will be reported as unverifiable, send Letter #13 along with a copy of Insert J which has been returned to you from the company with a company representative's signature. The letter and insert you will send to the credit agency will be the same as if you found incorrect account information on your credit report. The credit agency will do its reinvestigation into the account by contacting the organization. In the letter you sent to the credit agency is the name of the person you contacted at the organization. He or she will tell the credit agency that the account never existed or is unverifiable and should be removed from your credit report.

KNOWING WHERE TO SEND YOUR LETTERS

Regardless of which letters you send, knowing where to send them is important. Check this easy reference chart to determine where your letters should be sent.

Agency	Address	Phone Number
Trans-Union	Address is located at the end of your credit report	Phone number is located at the end of your credit report
Equifax	Research Requests Equifax Credit Informational Service P.O. Box 740241 Atlanta, GA 30374	(800) 210-3435
Experian	Experian P.O. Box 2106 Allen, TX 75013-2106	(800) 422-4879

(Be sure to check your credit report for addresses and phone numbers that are different from the ones above; information may change.)

Chapter 9

The Follow-Up Letters

THE FIRST FOLLOW-UP LETTERS

You now have had the chance to determine your credit difficulties and send out the appropriate letters. At this point, you have done more than the average person does when attempting to strengthen their credit. And although all of the work you have completed up to now may have seemed difficult, the most important part is yet to come.

The most important aspect of the strengthening process is following up your efforts. In order for all of your hard work to be successful, you must follow up every request you make. Following up on your requests shows your dedication to getting your credit back on the right track.

The follow-up process is a necessary step, helping to ensure everything is going smoothly. Take sales, for example. In sales, the sales process does not end once the customer says, "Yes, I'll take it." The most important part of a salesperson's job is the follow-up process. Any good salesperson would say that by following up, they're increasing their chances of having the customer return. And as a consumer, we feel closer to the salesperson if they keep in touch with us. Keeping in contact helps to ensure you will not be forgotten.

In order for you to succeed in strengthening your credit, the follow-up process is critical. You must consider yourself as a salesperson trying to sell yourself to the lenders and credit agencies. Your success depends on making sure the lenders and credit agencies do not forget about you.

If you receive a reply back immediately that is to your satisfaction, sending a letter of gratitude is acceptable. Use Letter #23 from Appendix B if you receive an immediate reply from a credit agency. Use Letter #24 if you receive an immediate reply from a company detailing an appropriate payment plan. And use Letter #25 if you receive an immediate reply from a company stating they will help maintain your good credit rating.

If you do not get a response from your original letter after waiting what you stated in your letter to be a "reasonable time period," you need to send a follow-up letter. The first follow-up letter is just going to be a reminder to whomever you sent it to that you have not heard from them yet. The follow-up letter is going to be firm, but not disrespectful, restating the facts of the matter. The letter will simply let the receiver be aware that a letter was sent to them and they failed to respond.

Each of the original 22 sample letters has a follow-up letter already prepared to coincide. Depending on the nature of your original letter, you need to choose the appropriate follow-up letter. Just look at the following table to match the follow-up letter with the original letter that you sent. All of the follow-up letters are located in Appendix B.

When sending the follow-up letters, be sure you send them to the same address as the original letters.

First Follow-Up Letter Letter	Coincides with with Original Sample	First Follow-Up Letter Letter	Coincides with Original
# 23	Credit Agency	# 35	# 10
# 24	Company	# 36	# 11
# 25	Company	# 37	# 12
# 26	# 1	# 38	# 13
# 27	# 2	# 39	# 14
# 28	# 3	# 40	# 15
# 29	# 4	# 41	# 16
# 30	# 5	# 42	# 17
# 31	# 6	# 43	# 18
# 32	# 7	# 44	# 19
# 33	# 8	# 45	# 20
# 34	# 9	# 46	# 21 & # 22

(Numbers 23, 24, and 25 are letters of gratitude, to be sent only if you receive a quick and satisfactory response.)

THE FINAL FOLLOW-UP LETTERS

If you still get no response from your first follow-up letter, you will need to send a second follow-up letter.

The second follow-up letter is going to be more forceful and demanding, but still by no means rude or disrespectful. Remember, you are trying to get the receiver of the letter to respond in a favorable manner to your request. Being rude, disrespectful, or belligerent will lessen your chances of succeeding; remember the "human factor."

In the second follow-up letter, you will restate the issues you are concerned about, sending copies of all previous documentation. By sending the previous requests, you show that you have been trying to contact the receiver, and this is not just an attempt to fool them.

Since this letter is your final request, you must inform the receiver that you are aware of your legal rights should they choose to ignore your request. Remember, do not threaten! Providing concise and up-to-date information, you make their job easier. Let them know you can and will contact the appropriate agencies if necessary, such as the FTC and the BBB, along with any other organizations that are willing to assist.

As in all of your previous requests, you still need to insist the receiver involved send you documentation showing that your requests have been met.

Each of the first follow-up letters has a final follow-up letter prepared to coincide. Depending on the nature of your follow-up letter, you need to choose the appropriate final follow-up letter to send. Look at the table below when matching the final follow-up letter to the first follow-up letter that you sent. All of the final follow-up letters are located in Appendix C. When sending the final follow-up letters, be sure you send them to the same address as the follow-up letters.

Final Follow-Up Letter	Coincides with First Follow-Up Letter
# 47	# 26
# 48	# 27
# 49	# 28
# 50	# 29
# 51	# 30
# 52	# 31
# 53	# 32
# 54	# 33
# 55	# 34
# 56	# 35
# 57	# 36
# 58	# 37
# 59	# 38
# 60	# 39
# 61	# 40
# 62	# 41
# 63	# 42
# 64	# 43
# 65	# 44
# 66	# 45
# 67	# 46

Chapter 10

Other Alternatives Available

Despite what anyone says, you have the right to dispute anything you believe is inaccurate on your credit report. However, not all lenders and credit agencies hold the same beliefs. If you find your requests go unanswered after exhausting all efforts to straighten out your credit through the methods provided, alternative actions may be necessary. There are several alternative actions that you may take:

Alternatives Available to You

A   Contact the Federal Trade Commission

B   Contact the Better Business Bureau

C   Contact other government agencies

D   Contact other support groups

E   Add a consumer statement to your credit report

(Don't give up too soon; contacting the lender or credit agency is still your best bet.)

CONTACTING THE FEDERAL TRADE COMMISSION

One alternative you have available is contacting the Federal Trade Commission (FTC). The commission's main function is to monitor businesses and credit agencies, making sure they are performing their duties, enforcing both federal antitrust laws and consumer protection laws. The FTC consists of a number of bureaus that are responsible for investigating and enforcing the laws.

The Bureau of Consumer Protection is the branch of the FTC that handles consumer credit issues. This branch is responsible for protecting consumers against unfair, deceptive, or fraudulent credit practices. The Bureau of Consumer Protection is broken down into five divisions:

Advertising Practices, Credit Practices, Enforcement, Marketing Practices, and Service Industry Practices. The division responsible for protecting the consumer is the Division of Credit Practices. This division is responsible for enforcing several of the statutes that protect the consumer, such as those listed here.

Statutes Enforced by the Division of Credit Practices

1   The Equal Credit Opportunity Act
2   The Fair Credit Reporting Act
3   The Truth in Lending Act
4   The Fair Credit Billing Act and The Electronic Fund Transfer Act
5   The Consumer Leasing Act
6   The Fair Debt Collection Practices Act
7   The Holder-In-Due-Course Rule
8   The Credit Practices Rule

In the final follow-up letters, the FTC is used as a final attention-getter. In many instances lenders and credit reporting agencies will avoid any dealings with the FTC. So before contacting the FTC, wait a reasonable amount of time. Then if you do not get a reply, go ahead and contact the FTC.

In the United States there are 10 regional branch offices of the FTC, with the national office located in Washington, D.C. Each regional branch office is responsible for certain states. Contact information for the 10 branch offices and the national office follows.

Regional Branch	Address	Phone & Fax	States
Atlanta	Federal Trade Commission 60 Forsyth St. SW, Ste. 5M35 Atlanta, GA 30303-2322	P: (404) 656-2322, F: (404) 656-1379	AL, FL, GA, MS, NC, SC, TN, VA
Boston	Federal Trade Commission 10 Merrimac St., Ste. 810 Boston, MA 02144-4719	P: (617) 424-5960, F: (617) 424-55998	CT, ME, MA, NH, RI, VT
Chicago	Federal Trade Commission 55 E. Monroe St., Ste. 1860 Chicago, IL 60603-5701	P: (312) 960-5633, F: (312) 960-5600	IL, IN, IA, KY, MN, MO, WI
Cleveland	Federal Trade Commission 1111 Superior Ave., Ste. 200 Cleveland, OH 44114-2507	P: (216) 263-3410, F: (216) 263-3426	DE, MD, MI, OH, PA, WA, District of Columbia
Dallas	Federal Trade Commission 1999 Bryan St., Ste. 2150 Dallas, TX 75201-6808	P: (214) 979-0213, F: N/A	AK, LA, NM, OK, TX
Denver	Federal Trade Commission 1961 Stout St., Ste. 1523 Denver, CO 80294-0101	P: (303) 844-2271, F: N/A	CO, KS, MT, NE, ND, SD, UT, WY
Los Angeles	Federal Trade Commission 10877 Wilshire Blvd., Ste. 700 Los Angeles, CA 90024	P: (310) 824-4300, F: N/A	AZ, Southern CA
New York	Federal Trade Commission 150 William St., Ste. 1300 New York, NY 10038	P: (212) 264-1207, F: (212) 264-0459	NJ, NY
San Francisco	Federal Trade Commission 910 Market St., Ste. 570 San Francisco, CA 94103	P: (415) 356-5270, F: (415) 356-5284	HI, NV, Northern CA
Seattle	Federal Trade Commission 2806 Federal Bldg. 915 Second Ave. Seattle, WA 98174	P: (206) 220-6363, F: (206) 220-6366	AL, ID, OR, WA

National Office	Address	Phone & Fax	States
Washington D.C.	Federal Trade Commission CRC-240 Washington, D.C. 20580	(877) 382-4537	N/A

For more information about the Federal Trade Commission contact their Web site at **www.ftc.gov.**

CONTACTING THE BBB

The Better Business Bureau provides you with another outlet for you to use in the event of unfair treatment. The BBB is a private, nonprofit organization that is supported mainly by membership dues paid by businesses and professional groups within the BBB's service location. The BBB provides the community with:

1. Reports on businesses to help the consumer make better-informed decisions when purchasing.
2. Information regarding charity groups and organizations.
3. Consumer dispute resolutions with businesses via telephone conciliation, mediation, and arbitration.
4. Ethical business standards and voluntary self-regulation of practices.

There are over 130 BBB's located throughout the United States. If you have a dispute with a business and you feel the BBB can help, contact the BBB where the business is located. In order to locate the BBB nearest you, check your local phone directory or call directory information. Once you contact the nearest BBB, they can direct you to the correct branch.

For more information regarding the Better Business Bureau contact their Web site *www.bbb.org.*

CONTACTING OTHER GOVERNMENT AGENCIES

There are several other government agencies with the authority to enforce the FCRA. Depending on what area you are dealing with, you can contact one or all of the following:

Government Agency	Areas Covered	Address	Phone Number
Office of the Comptroller of the Currency	National banks, federal branches/ agencies of foreign banks (the word "National"or initials "N.A." appear after bank's name).	Office of the of the Currency Compliance Management, Mail Stop 6-6 Washington, DC 20219	(800) 613-6743
Federal Reserve Board	Federal Reserve System member banks (except national banks and federal branches/agencies of foreign banks).	Federal Reserve Board Division of Consumer & Community Affairs Washington, DC 20551	(202) 452-3693
Office of Thrift Supervision	Savings associations and federally chartered savings banks (the word "Federal" or initials "F.S.B." appear in a federal institution's name).	Office of Thrift Supervision Consumer Programs Washington, DC 20552	(800) 842-6929
National Credit Union Administration	Federal credit unions (the words "Federal Credit Union" appear in the institution's name).	National Credit Union Administration 1775 Duke St. Alexandria, VA 22314	(703) 518-6360
Federal Deposit Insurance Corporation	State-chartered banks that are not members of the Federal Reserve System.	Federal Deposit Insurance Corporation Division of Compliance & Consumer Affairs Washington, DC 20429	(800) 934-3232
Department of Transportation	Air, surface, or rail common carriers regulated by former Civil Aeronautics Board or Interstate Commerce Commission.	Department of Transportation Office of Financial Management Washington, DC 20590	(202) 366-1306
Department of Agriculture	Activities subject to the Packers and Stockyards Act, 1921.	Department of Agriculture Office of Deputy Administrator-GIPSA Washington, DC 20250	(202) 720-7051

CONTACTING OTHER ORGANIZATIONS

Along with the FTC, BBB, and the other governmental agencies, there are also several other support groups you can contact. Depending on the circumstances, you can contact one or all of the following:

Organization	Description of Organization	Phone Number & Web Address
BankCard Holders of America	Nonprofit consumer protection organization whose main function is to protect the rights and interests of credit card consumers. The organization also monitors the current economic trends and changing events in the banking segment to determine how these trends and changes will effect consumers	P: (540) 389-5445, W: N/A
Call For Action	Worldwide support group of volunteers who use television and radio to educate, coach, and problem solve for consumers and small businesses.	P: (301) 657-7490, W: N/A
Debt Counselors of America	Nonprofit consumer assistance group that uses the Internet to help consumers worldwide. The site provides free information, shareware, and an on-line debt forum.	P: (800)680-3328, W: *www.DCA.org*
National Foundation for Consumer Credit	Nonprofit credit counseling organization that works to help consumers comprehend credit reports, contact creditors, manage debts, comprehend debts, and set up budgets.	P: (800) 388-2227, W: *www.CCCINTL.org*

ADDING A CONSUMER STATEMENT

Finally, if you feel you have exhausted all of your options, or that your current or past credit issues need to be explained, add a consumer statement. Consumer reporting agencies, by law, must allow you to add a consumer statement to your credit report explaining any credit issues you feel need to be clarified. The only restriction to adding a consumer statement is that it must consist of 100 words or less.

If you decide to add a consumer statement to your credit report, put some thought into what you want to say. Because you only have 100 words to work with, you want to choose your words wisely. By sticking just to the facts, you increase the reliability, validity, and effectiveness of the statement.

There are times when adding a consumer statement could actually be detrimental to your situation. You do not want to add a consumer statement if you are in the middle of disputing the credit information. If you immediately add a consumer statement, the information you are disputing could come back in your favor, and then you have a statement on your report detailing a problem that does not exist. The only thing the consumer statement has done, in this case, is to alert future creditors that there may be a potential problem.

Since writing a concise statement is important, here are a few examples of consumer statements to help you get started:

Example 1

The first example explains circumstances affecting the ability to pay debts. For instance, let's say you were in a bad accident and your insurance lapsed. You recovered, but the hospital bills started to pile up, making them impossible to pay. In this example, you had the forthrightness to contact the hospital to explain your situation, and you were able to set up a payment plan with the hospital in which you were making small monthly payments. Somehow, despite the agreement, your account was turned over to a collection agency. Let's say you have gone through all of the channels and no one has been able to help you. A consumer statement might say the following:

> In 1992 I was in a bad motorcycle accident. Unfortunately, due to a technicality I had no medical insurance at the time. Raising a family, I could not pay the accumulating hospital bills on time. I arranged a payment plan with the hospital, but the hospital still turned my account over for collection. I am a responsible consumer, which you can see by my other accounts. I have since recovered from the accident, and I am working full time.

Example 2

The second example deals with the same scenario as example one, only let's say you did not contact the hospital to set up a payment plan. You can still submit a consumer statement stating what you have gone through. Your consumer statement should concentrate more on the details surrounding the accident and why you could not make the payments. A consumer statement might say the following:

> *In 1992 I was in a bad motorcycle accident. Unfortunately, due to a technicality I had no medical insurance at the time. With the high costs of hospital stays, recovery, and physical therapy accumulating, I could not pay the hospital bills on time and raise a family. I am a responsible consumer, which you can see by my other accounts. I have since recovered from the accident and am working full time and paying back the hospital.*

It is important to get to the point, state the facts, and be honest. When adding a consumer statement such as the ones in Examples 1 and 2, use Letter #21 from Appendix A.

Example 3

The third example of a consumer statement explains inaccurate information that was reported to your credit report. Despite all of your efforts to have the information corrected, the information has not been removed from your credit report. A consumer statement might say the following:

> *On my credit report there is a JC Penney's account that is being reported as a bad account. I have never had a JC Penney's account in my name, nor have I signed with another person. I have tried to remove the account from my records, but nothing has changed. Please disregard this account when making a decision regarding my credit worthiness. Thank you.*

When adding a consumer statement to clarify incorrect information on your credit report, use Letter #22 from Appendix A.

KNOWING WHERE TO SEND YOUR LETTERS

Regardless of which letters you send, knowing where to send them is important. Check the easy reference chart below to determine where your letters should be sent.

Agency	Address	Phone Number
Trans-Union	Address is located at the end of your credit report	Phone number is located at the end of your credit report
Equifax	Research Requests Equifax Credit Information Service P.O. Box 740241 Atlanta, GA 30374	(800) 210-3435
Experian	Experian P.O.Box 2106 Allen, TX 75013-2106	(800) 422-4879

(Be sure to check your credit report for addresses and phone numbers that are different from the ones above; information may change.)

Chapter 11

Off You Go

A lot of useful information has been placed at your fingertips. All of it is prepared to help you get results. Now, all you have to do is put the information to work for you. What you do with the information and how diligent you are in following through will determine your success.

Schedule a day where you can sit down and go over the material. By putting your intentions on your calendar, you're increasing your likelihood of actually sitting down and beginning. Try to give yourself a couple of hours to go through the information. But by all means take your time, and if you run out of time don't worry, just leave yourself a note, and come back a little later—even a half-hour a day can help.

Your credit, regardless of what people may think, is a valuable asset. Try to think about your credit as a new car. If you polish, maintain, and service your car, the car will stay in good condition, providing you with a reliable means for transportation. The same principle holds true for your credit. If you update, add, delete, and keep your accounts good, your credit will stay in good condition, providing you with endless financial opportunities.

Pat yourself on the back and congratulate yourself for taking a stand. You are on the brink of putting your credit back on the right track. Avoiding your bad credit problems will not make them go away, and it could make the problem worse, so taking steps now is the best decision you could make for your financial future.

Your credit will be good again one day. Fix your past credit problems and then forget about them. The future is much more important. Every time you pay a bill, loan, or debt on time you are strengthening your credit. A lender is more interested in what you have done during the last two years than what you did five years ago. Start strengthening your credit today!

Original Letters

The easy reference chart below allows you to find at a glance the Original Letter you will be using.

Original Letter #	Description
1	Yearly Free Report
2	Applicable Fee
3	Denial of Credit
4	Denial of Employment
5	Denial of Insurance
6	Denial of Rental Housing
7	Unemployed Seeking Employment
8	Victim of Fraud
9	Public Assistance Recipient
10	Updating Information on Credit Report
11	Adding New Accounts to Credit Report
12	Making a Late Payment (one time)
13	Account Does Not Belong to Me (1)
14	You Can't Make the Monthly Payments (1)
15	You Can't Make the Monthly Payments (2)
16	Account Does Not Belong to Me (2)
17	Account Is Too Old
18	Inquiry Is Too Old
19	Consumer Statement Is Too Old
20	Account Will Be Paid In Full, If . . .
21	Adding a Consumer Statement (1)
22	Adding a Consumer Statement (2)

REASON 1: YEARLY FREE REPORT   *Original Letter 1*

Name / Date

Address 1

Address 2

Home and Work Phone

Social Security Number

I, (Mr./Mrs./Ms.) (Your Full Name), request a complimentary copy of my complete credit report.

This request is in accordance with state regulations and the Fair Credit Reporting Act of 1970, which states the credit agency must provide me with a complimentary copy of my credit report once a year, upon request, at no charge.

Please send a complete complimentary copy of my credit report to the address provided above. To help ensure that the correct report is generated, the following additional information is provided:

Date of Birth:_____

Previous Names (aliases, previous marriages, name changes, or name shortenings):

_____

_____

Previous   Addresses   and   Employers
(if you have been at your current address or employment for less than five years):

_____

_____

Spouse's First Name (if you are married):_____

Thank you for your cooperation.

Sincerely,

(Sign your name)

(Print your name)

Enclosures: Copy of Driver's License/Copy of Current Utility Bill

REASON 1: APPLICABLE FEE   *Original Letter 2*

Name / Date
Address 1
Address 2
Home and Work Phone
Social Security Number

I, (Mr./Mrs./Ms.) (Your Full Name), request a copy of my complete credit report.

Included is the fee of $_____ + tax, which is the cost you have set for generating this credit report.

To help ensure that the correct report is generated, the following additional information is provided:

Date of Birth:_____

Previous Names (aliases, previous marriages, name changes, or name shortenings):
_____
_____

Previous   Addresses   and   Employers
(if you have been at your current address or employment for less than five years):
_____
_____

Spouse's First Name (if you are married):_____

Thank you for your cooperation.

Sincerely,

(Sign your name)

(Print your name)

Enclosures: Copy of Driver's License/Copy of Current Utility Bill/
Check for Applicable Fee

REASON 2: DENIAL OF CREDIT   *Original Letter 3*

Name / Date

Address 1

Address 2

Home and Work Phone

Social Security Number

I, (Mr./Mrs./Ms.) (Your Full Name), request a complimentary copy of my complete credit report.

Your credit report was used in the evaluation of my credit worthiness and my request for credit was denied. I have enclosed a copy of the letter stating that I have been denied for credit.

This request is in accordance with the Fair Credit Reporting Act of 1970, which states the credit agency must provide me with a complimentary copy of my credit report, based on the denial of credit, upon request, at no charge.

Please send a complete complimentary copy of my credit report to the address provided above. To help ensure that the correct report is generated, the following additional information is provided:

Date of Birth: _____

Previous Names (aliases, previous marriages, name changes, or name shortenings):

_____

_____

Previous   Addresses   and   Employers
(if you have been at your current address or employment for less than five years):

_____

_____

Spouse's First Name (if you are married): _____

Thank you for your cooperation.

Sincerely,

(Sign your name)

(Print your name)

Enclosures: Letter of Denial of Credit/Copy of Driver's License/
Copy of Current Utility Bill

REASON 2: DENIAL OF EMPLOYMENT   *Original Letter 4*

Name / Date
Address 1
Address 2
Home and Work Phone
Social Security Number

I, (Mr./Mrs./Ms.) (Your Full Name), request a complimentary copy of my complete credit report.

Your credit report was used in consideration of my application for employment and the evaluation of my credit worthiness. I was denied employment based on information gathered in the hiring process. I have enclosed a copy of the letter stating that I have been denied employment.

This request is in accordance with the Fair Credit Reporting Act of 1970, which states the credit agency must provide me with a complimentary copy of my credit report, based on the denial of employment, upon request, at no charge.

Please send a complete complimentary copy of my credit report to the address provided above. To help ensure that the correct report is generated, the following additional information is provided:

Date of Birth: _____

Previous Names (aliases, previous marriages, name changes, or name shortenings):
_____
_____

Previous   Addresses   and   Employers
(if you have been at your current address or employment for less than five years):
_____
_____

Spouse's First Name (if you are married): _____

Thank you for your cooperation.
Sincerely,
(Sign your name)
(Print your name)

Enclosures: Letter of Denial of Employment/Copy of Driver's License/ Copy of Current Utility Bill

REASON 2: DENIAL OF INSURANCE   *Original Letter 5*

Name / Date

Address 1

Address 2

Home and Work Phone

Social Security Number

I, (Mr./Mrs./Ms.) (Your Full Name), request a complimentary copy of my complete credit report.

Your credit report was used in consideration of my application for insurance and the evaluation of my credit worthiness. I was denied insurance based on information gathered during the screening process. I have enclosed a copy of the letter stating that I have been denied insurance.

This request is in accordance with the Fair Credit Reporting Act of 1970, which states the credit agency must provide me with a complimentary copy of my credit report, based on the denial of insurance, upon request, at no charge.

Please send a complete complimentary copy of my credit report to the address provided above. To help ensure that the correct report is generated, the following additional information is provided:

Date of Birth: _____

Previous Names (aliases, previous marriages, name changes, or name shortenings):

_____

_____

Previous   Addresses   and   Employers
(if you have been at your current address or employment for less than five years):

_____

_____

Spouse's First Name (if you are married): _____

Thank you for your cooperation.
Sincerely,
(Sign your name)
(Print your name)

Enclosures: Letter of Denial of Employment/Copy of Driver's License/
Copy of Current Utility Bill

REASON 2: DENIAL OF RENTAL HOUSING   *Original Letter 6*

Name / Date
Address 1
Address 2
Home and Work Phone
Social Security Number

I, (Mr./Mrs./Ms.) (Your Full Name), request a complimentary copy of my complete credit report.

Your credit report was used in consideration of my application for rental housing and the evaluation of my credit worthiness. I was denied rental housing based on information gathered during the background process. I have enclosed a copy of the letter stating that I have been denied rental housing.

This request is in accordance with the Fair Credit Reporting Act of 1970, which states the credit agency must provide me with a complimentary copy of my credit report, based on the denial of rental housing, upon request, at no charge.

Please send a complete complimentary copy of my credit report to the address provided above. To help ensure that the correct report is generated, the following additional information is provided:

Date of Birth:_____

Previous Names (aliases, previous marriages, name changes, or name shortenings):

_____

_____

Previous   Addresses   and   Employers
(if you have been at your current address or employment for less than five years):

_____

_____

Spouse's First Name (if you are married):_____

Thank you for your cooperation.
Sincerely,
(Sign your name)
(Print your name)

Enclosures: Letter of Denial of Employment/Copy of Driver's License/
Copy of Current Utility Bill

REASON 3: UNEMPLOYED, SEEKING EMPLOYMENT   *Original Letter 7*

Name / Date

Address 1

Address 2

Home and Work Phone

Social Security Number

I, (Mr./Mrs./Ms.) (Your Full Name), request a complimentary copy of my complete credit report.

I am currently unemployed and will be seeking employment within the next 60 days.

This request is in accordance with the Fair Credit Reporting Act of 1970, which states the credit agency must provide me with a complimentary copy of my credit report, based on being unemployed and seeking employment within 60 days, upon request, at no charge.

Please send a complete complimentary copy of my credit report to the address provided above. To help ensure that the correct report is generated, the following additional information is provided:

Date of Birth:_____

Previous Names (aliases, previous marriages, name changes, or name shortenings):

_____

_____

Previous   Addresses   and   Employers
(if you have been at your current address or employment for less than five years):

_____

_____

Spouse's First Name (if you are married):_____

Thank you for your cooperation.

Sincerely,

(Sign your name)

(Print your name)

Enclosures: Copy of Driver's License/Copy of Current Utility Bill

REASON 3: VICTIM OF FRAUD   *Original Letter 8*

Name / Date
Address 1
Address 2
Home and Work Phone
Social Security Number

I, (Mr./Mrs./Ms.) (Your Full Name), request a complimentary copy of my complete credit report.

I believe that I have been a victim of credit fraud.

This request is in accordance with the Fair Credit Reporting Act of 1970, which states the credit agency must provide me with a complimentary copy of my credit report, based on being a victim of credit fraud, upon request, at no charge.

Please send a complete complimentary copy of my credit report to the address provided above. To help ensure that the correct report is generated, the following additional information is provided:

Date of Birth: _____

Previous Names (aliases, previous marriages, name changes, or name shortenings):

_____

_____

Previous   Addresses   and   Employers
(if you have been at your current address or employment for less than five years):

_____

_____

Spouse's First Name (if you are married): _____

Thank you for your cooperation.

Sincerely,

(Sign your name)

(Print your name)

Enclosures: Copy of Driver's License/Copy of Current Utility Bill

REASON 3: PUBLIC ASSISTANCE RECIPIENT   *Original Letter 9*

Name / Date

Address 1

Address 2

Home and Work Phone

Social Security Number

I, (Mr./Mrs./Ms.) (Your Full Name), request a complimentary copy of my complete credit report.

I am currently a recipient of public assistance.

This request is in accordance with the Fair Credit Reporting Act of 1970, which states the credit agency must provide me with a complimentary copy of my credit report, based on being a recipient of public assistance, upon request, at no charge.

Please send a complete complimentary copy of my credit report to the address provided above. To help ensure that the correct report is generated, the following additional information is provided:

Date of Birth: _____

Previous Names (aliases, previous marriages, name changes, or name shortenings):

_____

_____

Previous   Addresses   and   Employers
(if you have been at your current address or employment for less than five years):

_____

_____

Spouse's First Name (if you are married): _____

Thank you for your cooperation.

Sincerely,

(Sign your name)

(Print your name)

Enclosures: Copy of Driver's License/Copy of Current Utility Bill

UPDATING INFORMATION ON YOUR CREDIT REPORT   *Original Letter 10*

Name / Date
Address 1
Address 2
Home and Work Phone
Social Security Number

I have recently acquired my credit report. After carefully reviewing its contents, I have found some information that needs to be updated.

I realize the importance, to both parties, of having an accurate credit report. Knowing this, please bring up to date the accounts listed on the enclosed insert(s), under the provisions of the Fair Credit Reporting Act (FCRA), 15 USC section 1681i. A period of 30 days shall be "reasonable time" to investigate and update the accounts in question, unless you notify me immediately otherwise.

Also, 15 USC sections 1681i(d) and 1681j of the Fair Credit Reporting Act require that I receive written notification of the appropriate corrections, an updated credit report (no charge), and an updated credit report be sent to anyone who received my report within the last six months.

Thank you for your cooperation.

Sincerely,

(Sign your name)

(Print your name)

Enclosures: (Update Account Insert)

ADDING NEW ACCOUNTS TO YOUR CREDIT REPORT   *Original Letter 11*

Name / Date
Address 1
Address 2
Home and Work Phone
Social Security Number

I have recently acquired my credit report to check the information that has been reported to it. After carefully reviewing my credit report, I have found there are accounts that are not being reported. I feel the accounts that are not being reported should be included on my credit report. I have included in this request the accounts I would like added to my credit report and the additional documentation supporting that these accounts are mine and are good accounts.

The Fair Credit Reporting Act (FCRA), 15 USC section 1681(b) clearly states: "It is the purpose of this title (FCRA) to require that consumer reporting agencies adopt reasonable procedures for meeting the needs of commerce for consumer credit, personnel, insurance, and other information in a manner which is fair and equitable to the consumer, with regard to the confidentiality, accuracy, relevancy, and proper utilization of such information in accordance with the requirements of this title." It is your responsibility according to the FCRA, as a consumer reporting agency, to add the additional accounts as requested.

Please update my credit report by adding the additional accounts requested to my trades and payment histories.

Please send a letter within 30 days stating that you have complied with the Fair Credit Reporting Act, 15 USC section 1681e, by updating my credit report. Also, send an updated credit report at no charge to the address listed above and to anyone who received my credit report within the last six months, according to 15 USC section 1681j.

Thank you for your cooperation.

Sincerely,

(Sign your name)

(Print your name)

Enclosures: (Add Account Insert/Account Documentation)

MAKING A LATE PAYMENT (ONE TIME)   *Original Letter 12*

Name / Date
Address 1
Address 2
Home and Work Phone
Social Security Number

Last month, due to uncontrollable circumstances, I was late in paying my account. As you can see from my past payments, this is an isolated incident and will not be a reoccurring practice.

Please realize that I understand the importance of maintaining good credit and the importance of maintaining a good credit rating with your company. Therefore, since this is an isolated incident and since my account is up to date, I would appreciate your cooperation in helping me protect my good credit.

I would appreciate your not reporting my account to the credit agencies as negative, rather as an on-time, good account. I have included an insert "H" which you can complete and send back to me. I will send this insert to the credit agency, who will in turn probably contact you during their investigation. Please provide me with the name of the person I can contact in order to set up this arrangement.

Once again, I realize the importance of having a good credit rating. Working together to rectify this situation will benefit us both. Please respond in writing within 30 days. If you have any further questions regarding this matter, you can contact me at home (000) 000-0000 or at work (000) 000-0000.

Thank you for your cooperation.

Sincerely,

(Sign your name)

(Print your name)

Enclosures: (Change My Credit Report Insert/Credit Report)

ACCOUNT DOES NOT BELONG TO ME   *Original Letter 13*

Name / Date
Address 1
Address 2
Home and Work Phone
Social Security Number

I have recently acquired my credit report. After carefully reviewing its contents, I have found some inaccurate information that the enclosed insert(s) and credit report detail.

I have contacted the organization in question. In order to verify this information you can speak with Mr./Ms. _____ at (000) 000-0000. He/She has been in charge of researching the account information.

Please investigate the accounts listed on the enclosed insert(s), under the provisions of the Fair Credit Reporting Act (FCRA), 15 USC section 1681i. A period of 30 days shall be "reasonable time" to investigate the accounts in question, unless you notify me immediately otherwise. Failure to verify the above information within the 30-day time period constitutes "non-verification" and the accounts in question must be immediately removed from my credit file and credit report according to 15 USC section 1681i(a).

Also, 15 USC sections 1681i(d) and 1681j of the Fair Credit Reporting Act require that I receive written notification of the appropriate corrections, an updated credit report (no charge), and an updated credit report be sent to anyone who received my report within the last six months.

Thank you for your cooperation.

Sincerely,

(Sign your name)

(Print your name)

Enclosures: (Change My Credit Report Insert/Delete Account from My Credit Report Insert/Credit Report)

CAN'T MAKE THE MONTHLY PAYMENT

Original Letter 14

Name / Date
Address 1
Address 2
Home and Work Phone
Social Security Number

Due to uncontrollable circumstances my account has become delinquent. As you can see from my past payments, this is not a regular occurrence.

Please realize that I understand the importance of maintaining good credit and the importance of maintaining a good credit rating with your company. Therefore, I would like to set up a payment plan to fulfill my responsibilities. The payment plan worksheet details the arrangements I would be able to handle at this time.

Since this incident is directly related to uncontrollable circumstances, I would appreciate your not reporting my account to the credit agencies as negative, rather as an on-time, good account. I have included an insert "H" that you can complete and send back to me. I will send this insert to the credit agency(ies), who will in turn probably contact you during their investigation. Please provide me with the name of the person I can contact in order to set up this arrangement.

Once again, I realize the importance of having a good credit rating. Working together to rectify this situation will benefit us both. Please respond in writing within 30 days. If you have any further questions regarding this matter, you can contact me at home (000) 000-0000 or at work (000) 000-0000.

Thank you for your cooperation.

Sincerely,

(Sign your name)

(Print your name)

Enclosures: (Payment Plan Insert/Change My Credit Report Insert)

CAN'T MAKE THE MONTHLY PAYMENTS

Original Letter 15

Name / Date

Address 1

Address 2

Home and Work Phone

Social Security Number

Due to uncontrollable circumstances my account has become delinquent. As you can see from my past payments, this is not a regular occurrence. I have included additional documentation that supports these uncontrollable circumstances.

Please realize that I understand the importance of maintaining good credit and the importance of maintaining a good credit rating with your company. Therefore, I would like to set up a payment plan to fulfill my responsibilities. The payment plan worksheet details the arrangements I would be able to handle at this time.

Since this incident is directly related to uncontrollable circumstances, I would appreciate your taking my account out of collection and reporting my account to the credit agencies as an on-time, good account. I have included an insert "H" that you can complete and send back to me. I will send this insert to the credit agency(ies), who will in turn probably contact you during their investigation. Please provide me with the name of the person I can contact in order to set up this arrangement.

Once again, I realize the importance of having a good credit rating. Working together to rectify this situation will benefit us both. Please respond in writing within 30 days. If you have any further questions regarding this matter, you can contact me at home (000) 000-0000 or at work (000) 000-0000.

Thank you for your cooperation.

Sincerely,

(Sign your name)

(Print your name)

Enclosures: (Payment Plan Insert/Change My Credit Report Insert)

ACCOUNT DOES NOT BELONG TO ME   *Original Letter 16*

Name / Date
Address 1
Address 2
Home and Work Phone
Social Security Number

I have recently acquired my credit report. After carefully reviewing its contents, I have found some inaccurate information that the enclosed insert(s) and credit report detail.

Please investigate the accounts listed on the enclosed insert(s), under the provisions of the Fair Credit Reporting Act (FCRA), 15 USC section 1681i. A period of 30 days shall be "reasonable time" to investigate the accounts in question, unless you notify me immediately otherwise. Failure to verify the above information within the 30-day time period constitutes "non-verification" and the accounts in question must be immediately removed from my credit file and credit report according to 15 USC section 1681i(a).

Also, 15 USC sections 1681i(d) and 1681j of the Fair Credit Reporting Act require that I receive written notification of the appropriate corrections, an updated credit report (no charge), and an updated credit report be sent to anyone who received my report within the last six months.

Thank you for your cooperation.

Sincerely,

(Sign your name)

(Print your name)

Enclosures: (Delete Account From My Credit Report Insert/Credit Report)

ACCOUNT IS TOO OLD   *Original Letter 17*

Name / Date
Address 1
Address 2
Home and Work Phone
Social Security Number

I have recently acquired my credit report. After carefully reviewing its contents, I have found some outdated account information that the enclosed insert(s) and credit report detail.

Please investigate the accounts listed on the enclosed insert(s), under the provisions of the Fair Credit Reporting Act (FCRA), 15 USC section 1681i. A period of 30 days shall be "reasonable time" to investigate the accounts in question, unless you notify me immediately otherwise. Failure to verify the above information within the 30-day time period constitutes "non-verification" and the accounts in question must be immediately removed from my credit file and credit report according to 15 USC section 1681i(a).

Also, 15 USC sections 1681i(d) and 1681j of the Fair Credit Reporting Act require that I receive written notification of the appropriate corrections, an updated credit report (no charge), and an updated credit report be sent to anyone who received my report within the last six months.

Thank you for your cooperation.

Sincerely,

(Sign your name)

(Print your name)

Enclosures: (Delete Old Account From My Credit Report Insert/Credit Report)

INQUIRY IS TOO OLD

Original Letter 18

Name / Date
Address 1
Address 2
Home and Work Phone
Social Security Number

I have recently acquired my credit report. After carefully reviewing its contents, I have found some outdated inquiry information that the enclosed insert(s) and credit report detail.

Please investigate the inquiries listed on the enclosed insert(s), under the provisions of the Fair Credit Reporting Act (FCRA), 15 USC section 1681i. A period of 30 days shall be "reasonable time" to investigate the inquiries in question, unless you notify me immediately otherwise. Failure to verify the above information within the 30-day time period constitutes "non-verification" and the inquiries in question must be immediately removed from my credit file and credit report according to 15 USC section 1681i(a).

Also, 15 USC sections 1681i(d) and 1681j of the Fair Credit Reporting Act require that I receive written notification of the appropriate corrections, an updated credit report (no charge), and an updated credit report be sent to anyone who received my report within the last six months.

Thank you for your cooperation.

Sincerely,

(Sign your name)

(Print your name)

Enclosures: (Delete Old Inquiry From My Credit Report Insert/Credit Report)

CONSUMER STATEMENT IS OLD

Original Letter 19

Name / Date
Address 1
Address 2
Home and Work Phone
Social Security Number

I have recently acquired my credit report. After carefully reviewing its contents, I have found some outdated consumer statement information that the enclosed insert(s) and credit report detail.

Please investigate the consumer statement listed on the enclosed insert(s), under the provisions of the Fair Credit Reporting Act (FCRA), 15 USC section 1681i. A period of 30 days shall be "reasonable time" to investigate the consumer statement in question, unless you notify me immediately otherwise. Failure to verify the above information within the 30-day time period constitutes "non-verification" and the consumer statement which is in question must be immediately removed from my credit file and credit report according to 15 USC section 1681i(a).

Also, 15 USC sections 1681i(d) and 1681j of the Fair Credit Reporting Act require that I receive written notification of the appropriate corrections, an updated credit report (no charge), and an updated credit report be sent to anyone who received my report within the last six months.

Thank you for your cooperation.

Sincerely,

(Sign your name)

(Print your name)

Enclosures: (Delete Old Consumer Statement From My Credit Report Insert/Credit Report)

ACCOUNT WILL BE PAID IN FULL, IF . . .   *Original Letter 20*

Name / Date
Address 1
Address 2
Home and Work Phone
Social Security Number

I have recently acquired my credit report. After carefully reviewing its contents, I am aware of an account with your organization that is appearing on my credit report as negative. I would like to settle this account.

The credit report states that I owe $_____. I will pay the full amount owed, if in return you will report my account as unverifiable to the credit agency.

Please provide me with the name of the person I can contact in order to set up this arrangement. This individual will also deal with the credit agency when they call to investigate the account.

I realize the importance of having a good credit rating. Working together to rectify this situation will benefit us both. Please respond in writing within 30 days. If you have any further questions regarding this matter, you can contact me at home (000) 000-0000 or at work (000) 000-0000.

Thank you for your cooperation.

Sincerely,

(Sign your name)

(Print your name)

Enclosures: (Delete Account from My Credit Report Insert)

ADDING A CONSUMER STATEMENT   *Original Letter 21*

Name / Date
Address 1
Address 2
Home and Work Phone
Social Security Number

I wish to add a Consumer Statement to my credit report, in accordance with the Fair Credit Reporting Act, 15 USC section 1681i(b).

Please add the following statement, word for word, to my credit report:

(Fill in statement.)

15 USC, sections 1681i(d) and 1681j of the Fair Credit Reporting Act require that I receive written notification of this addition to my credit report and an updated credit report at no charge to me. If you have any questions, please contact me at (000) 000-0000 (home) or (000) 000-0000 (work).

Thank you for your cooperation.

Sincerely,

(Sign your name)

(Print your name)

ADDING A CONSUMER STATEMENT   *Original Letter 22*

Name / Date
Address 1
Address 2
Home and Work Phone
Social Security Number

I wish to add a Consumer Statement to my credit report, in accordance with the Fair Credit Reporting Act, 15 USC section 1681i(b).

The investigation into items on my credit report I felt were inaccurate have not been verified. Included is a copy of my credit report with the items highlighted that I felt were inaccurate, along with a copy of all the letters I have sent trying to remedy the disputed information.

Please add the following statement, word for word, to my credit report:

(Fill in statement.)

15 USC, sections 1681i(d) and 1681j of the Fair Credit Reporting Act require that I receive written notification of this addition to my credit report and an updated credit report at no charge to me. If you have any questions, please contact me at (000) 000-0000 (home) or (000) 000-0000 (work).

Thank you for your cooperation.

Sincerely,

(Sign your name)

(Print your name)

Enclosures: (Original letter and insert, Follow-Up Letter, Second Follow-Up Letter, Driver's License)

Follow-Up Letters

The easy reference chart below allows you to find at a glance the Follow-Up Letter you will be using.

Follow-Up Letter #	Description
23	Agency Replies Promptly
24	Lender Replies Promptly (payment plan)
25	Lender Replies Promptly (good credit)
26	Yearly Free Report
27	Applicable Fee
28	Denial of Credit
29	Denial of Employment
30	Denial of Insurance
31	Denial of Rental Housing
32	Unemployed Seeking Employment
33	Victim of Fraud
34	Public Assistance Recipient
35	Updating Information on Credit Report
36	Adding New Accounts to Credit Report
37	Making a Late Payment (one time)
38	Account Does Not Belong To Me (1)
39	You Can't Make the Monthly Payments (1)
40	You Can't Make the Monthly Payments (2)
41	Account Does Not Belong to Me (2)
42	Account Is Too Old
43	Inquiry Is Too Old
44	Consumer Statement Is Too Old
45	Account Will Be Paid In Full, If . . .
46	Adding a Consumer Statement

WHEN AGENCY REPLIES PROMPTLY   *Follow-Up Letter 23*

Name / Date
Address 1
Address 2
Home and Work Phone
Social Security Number

On (Month/Day/Year), I sent a letter requesting your agency review items on my credit report that I felt were inaccurate.

Your agency, within a "reasonable time" period, investigated my concerns, and promptly removed the inaccurate information from my credit report.

I appreciate the timeliness and professionalism in which this matter was handled.

Keep up the great work.

Sincerely,

(Sign your name)

(Print your name)

WHEN LENDER REPLIES PROMPTLY (PAYMENT PLAN) *Follow-Up Letter 24*

Name / Date
Address 1
Address 2
Home and Work Phone
Social Security Number

On (Month/Day/Year) I sent a letter to your company in the hopes of maintaining our business relationship.

I dealt with Mr./Mrs. _____ from your organization.
Mr./Mrs._____ acted responsibly and professionally, helping me establish a payment plan that would satisfy both parties and at the same time maintain our business relationship. The matter at hand was respectfully and thoroughly handled.

I appreciate the timeliness and professionalism in which this matter was handled.

Keep up the great work.

Sincerely,

(Sign your name)

(Print your name)

WHEN LENDER REPLIES PROMPTLY (GOOD CREDIT) *Follow-Up Letter 25*

Name / Date

Address 1

Address 2

Home and Work Phone

Social Security Number

On (Month/Day/Year) I sent a letter to your company in the hopes of maintaining our business relationship.

I dealt with Mr./Mrs. _____ from your organization.
Mr./Mrs._____ acted responsibly and professionally, helping me maintain my positive credit rating with your company and the credit agencies. Due to the manner in which this situation was handled, I believe both parties have grown stronger while at the same time maintaining our business relationship.

I appreciate the timeliness and professionalism in which this matter was handled, and your dedication to maintaining our business relationship.

Keep up the great work.

Sincerely,

(Sign your name)

(Print your name)

FREE YEARLY REPORT

Follow-Up Letter 26

Name / Date
Address 1
Address 2
Home and Work Phone
Social Security Number

On (Month/Day/Year) I sent a letter to your agency requesting a complimentary copy of my credit report.

I have waited a "reasonable time" period for my request; however, my request has gone unanswered.

Once again, state regulations and the Fair Credit Reporting Act of 1970 allow me to receive a complimentary copy of my credit report once a year, upon request, at no charge.

Please send a complete complimentary copy of my credit report to the address provided above. I have included my original letter to assist you in expediting the process.

If you are having any difficulties completing this task, please contact me using the above information.

Thank you for your cooperation.

Sincerely,

(Sign your name)

(Print your name)

APPLICABLE FEE

Follow-Up Letter 27

Name / Date
Address 1
Address 2
Home and Work Phone
Social Security Number

On (Month/Day/Year) I sent a letter to your agency requesting a copy of my credit report. Along with my request was a check in the amount of $_____, in payment for the cost of generating the report.

I have waited a "reasonable time" period for my request; however, my request has gone unanswered.

Once again, state regulations and the Fair Credit Reporting Act of 1970 allow me to receive a copy of my credit report, upon request, as frequently as I wish.

Please send a complete copy of my credit report to the address provided above. I have included my original letter to assist you in expediting the process. If you are having any difficulties completing this task, please contact me using the above information.

Thank you for your cooperation.

Sincerely,

(Sign your name)

(Print your name)

DENIAL OF CREDIT

Follow-Up Letter 28

Name / Date
Address 1
Address 2
Home and Work Phone
Social Security Number

On (Month/Day/Year) I sent a letter to your agency requesting a complimentary copy of my credit report due to your agency's credit report being used in determining my denial for credit.

I have waited a "reasonable time" period for my request; however, my request has gone unanswered.

Once again, state regulations and the Fair Credit Reporting Act of 1970 allow me to receive a complimentary copy of my credit report, if denied credit, at no cost to me.

Please send a complete complimentary copy of my credit report to the address provided above. I have included the original letter, which I sent, to assist you in expediting the process.

If you are having any difficulties completing this task, please contact me using the above information.

Thank you for your cooperation.

Sincerely,

(Sign your name)

(Print your name)

DENIAL OF EMPLOYMENT

Follow-Up Letter 29

Name / Date
Address 1
Address 2
Home and Work Phone
Social Security Number

On (Month/Day/Year) I sent a letter to your agency requesting a complimentary copy of my credit report due to your agency's credit report being used in determining my denial for employment.

I have waited a "reasonable time" period for my request; however, my request has gone unanswered.

Once again, state regulations and the Fair Credit Reporting Act of 1970 allow me to receive a complimentary copy of my credit report, if denied employment, at no cost to me.

Please send a complete complimentary copy of my credit report to the address provided above. I have included my original letter to assist you in expediting the process.

If you are having any difficulties completing this task, please contact me using the above information.

Thank you for your cooperation.

Sincerely,

(Sign your name)

(Print your name)

DENIAL OF INSURANCE

Follow-Up Letter 30

Name / Date

Address 1

Address 2

Home and Work Phone

Social Security Number

On (Month/Day/Year) I sent a letter to your agency requesting a complimentary copy of my credit report due to your agency's credit report being used in determining my denial for insurance.

I have waited a "reasonable time" period for my request; however, my request has gone unanswered.

Once again, state regulations and the Fair Credit Reporting Act of 1970 allow me to receive a complimentary copy of my credit report, if denied insurance, at no cost to me.

Please send a complete complimentary copy of my credit report to the address provided above. I have included my original letter to assist you in expediting the process.

If you are having any difficulties completing this task, please contact me using the above information.

Thank you for your cooperation.

Sincerely,

(Sign your name)

(Print your name)

DENIAL OF RENTAL HOUSING

Follow-Up Letter 31

Name / Date
Address 1
Address 2
Home and Work Phone
Social Security Number

On (Month/Day/Year) I sent a letter to your agency requesting a complimentary copy of my credit report due to your agency's credit report being used in determining my denial for rental housing.

I have waited a "reasonable time" period for my request; however, my request has gone unanswered.

Once again, state regulations and the Fair Credit Reporting Act of 1970 allow me to receive a complimentary copy of my credit report, if denied rental housing, at no cost to me.

Please send a complete complimentary copy of my credit report to the address provided above. I have included my original letter to assist you in expediting the process.

If you are having any difficulties completing this task, please contact me using the above information.

Thank you for your cooperation.

Sincerely,

(Sign your name)

(Print your name)

UNEMPLOYED, SEEKING EMPLOYMENT

Follow-Up Letter 32

Name / Date
Address 1
Address 2
Home and Work Phone
Social Security Number

On (Month/Day/Year) I sent a letter to your agency requesting a complimentary copy of my credit report due to my being unemployed and seeking employment.

I have waited a "reasonable time" period for my request; however, my request has gone unanswered.

Once again, state regulations and the Fair Credit Reporting Act of 1970 allow me to receive a complimentary copy of my credit report, if I am unemployed seeking employment, at no cost to me.

Please send a complete complimentary copy of my credit report to the address provided above. I have included my original letter to assist you in expediting the process.

If you are having any difficulties completing this task, please contact me using the above information.

Thank you for your cooperation.

Sincerely,

(Sign your name)

(Print your name)

VICTIM OF FRAUD *Follow-Up Letter 33*

Name / Date
Address 1
Address 2
Home and Work Phone
Social Security Number

On (Month/Day/Year) I sent a letter to your agency requesting a complimentary copy of my credit report due to my being a victim of fraud.

I have waited a "reasonable time" period for my request; however, my request has gone unanswered.

Once again, state regulations and the Fair Credit Reporting Act of 1970 allow me to receive a complimentary copy of my credit report, if I a victim of fraud, at no cost to me.

Please send a complete complimentary copy of my credit report to the address provided above. I have included my original letter to assist you in expediting the process.

If you are having any difficulties completing this task, please contact me using the above information.

Thank you for your cooperation.

Sincerely,

(Sign your name)

(Print your name)

PUBLIC ASSISTANCE RECIPIENT

Follow-Up Letter 34

Name / Date
Address 1
Address 2
Home and Work Phone
Social Security Number

On (Month/Day/Year) I sent a letter to your agency requesting a complimentary copy of my credit report due to my being a public assistance recipient.

I have waited a "reasonable time" period for my request; however, my request has gone unanswered.

Once again, state regulations and the Fair Credit Reporting Act of 1970 allow me to receive a complimentary copy of my credit report, if I am a public assistance recipient, at no cost to me.

Please send a complete complimentary copy of my credit report to the address provided above. I have included my original letter to assist you in expediting the process.

If you are having any difficulties completing this task, please contact me using the above information.

Thank you for your cooperation.

Sincerely,

(Sign your name)

(Print your name)

UPDATING INFORMATION ON CREDIT REPORT   *Follow-Up Letter 35*

Name / Date

Address 1

Address 2

Home and Work Phone

Social Security Number

On (Month/Day/Year) I sent a letter to your agency requesting that information posted to my credit report be updated; however, my request has gone unanswered.

My original letter stated that a 30-day time period would constitute "reasonable time" for the updating of my credit report, as mandated by the Fair Credit Reporting Act.

Once again, I realize the importance, to both parties, of having an accurate credit report. Knowing this, please investigate and bring the information listed on the enclosed insert up to date on my credit report and file.

Also, 15 USC sections 1681i(d) and 1681j of the Fair Credit Reporting Act require that I receive written notification of the updates, an up-to-date credit report (at no charge), and that an up-to-date credit report be sent to anyone who received my credit report within the last six months.

Thank you for your cooperation.

Sincerely,

(Sign your name)

(Print your name)

ADDING NEW ACCOUNTS TO CREDIT REPORT   *Follow-Up Letter 36*

Name / Date
Address 1
Address 2
Home and Work Phone
Social Security Number

On (Month/Day/Year) I sent a letter to your agency requesting that additional credit information be added to my credit report. My original letter stated that a 30-day time period would constitute "reasonable time" for the adding of these accounts to my credit report; however, my request has gone unanswered.

Once again, I realize the importance, to both parties, of having a complete and accurate credit report. Knowing this, please investigate and add the information listed on the enclosed insert to my credit report and file.

Also, 15 USC sections 1681i(d) and 1681j of the Fair Credit Reporting Act require that I receive written notification of the updates, an up-to-date credit report (at no charge), and that an up-to-date credit report be sent to anyone who received my credit report within the last six months.

If you are having any difficulties completing this task, please contact me using the above information.

Thank you for your cooperation.

Sincerely,

(Sign your name)

(Print your name)

MAKING A LATE PAYMENT (ONE TIME)   *Follow-Up Letter 37*

Name / Date
Address 1
Address 2
Home and Work Phone
Social Security Number

On (Month/Day/Year) I sent a letter to your company explaining the reasons behind my making a late payment. I asked if you would respond within a month's time; however, a month has passed and I have not heard back from anyone regarding this matter.

Once again, I realize the importance, to both parties, of maintaining a good credit rating.

Knowing this, I had asked for your help in protecting my credit rating by not reporting my account to the credit agencies as negative.

I am including a copy of my original letter with this letter. Please provide me with the name of the person I can contact in order to set up this arrangement. If you have any further questions regarding this matter, you can contact me at the numbers listed above.

Thank you for your cooperation.

Sincerely,

(Sign your name)

(Print your name)

THIS ACCOUNT DOES NOT BELONG TO ME   *Follow-Up Letter 38*

Name / Date
Address 1
Address 2
Home and Work Phone
Social Security Number

On (Month/Day/Year) I sent a letter to your agency requesting the investigation and removal of inaccurate account information from my credit report. I asked if you would respond within a month's time; however, a month has passed and I have not heard back from anyone regarding this matter.

I have been in contact with Mr./Mrs._____, from (Name of Company), the person who is in charge of this matter. Mr./Mrs._____ can be contacted at (000) 000-0000.

Once again, please investigate the accounts listed on the enclosed insert(s), under the provisions of the Fair Credit Reporting Act, 15 USC section 1681i. If the information I requested to be investigated is found to be inaccurate, all items that fall under this investigation must be removed immediately from my credit report and file.

Also, 15 USC sections 1681i(d) and 1681j of the Fair Credit Reporting Act require that I receive written notification of the updates, an up-to-date credit report (at no charge), and that an up-to-date credit report be sent to anyone who received my credit report within the last six months.

If you are having any difficulties completing this task, please contact me using the above information.

Thank you for your cooperation.

Sincerely,

(Sign your name)

(Print your name)

YOU CAN'T MAKE THE MONTHLY PAYMENTS   *Follow-Up Letter 39*

Name / Date
Address 1
Address 2
Home and Work Phone
Social Security Number

On (Month/Day/Year) I sent a letter to your company explaining the reasons behind my having difficulties making my monthly payment and setting up a payment plan. I asked if you would respond within a month's time; however, a month has passed and I have not heard back from anyone regarding this matter.

Once again, I realize the importance, to both parties, of maintaining a good credit rating.

Knowing this, I have asked for your help in setting up a payment plan, so that I may fulfill my responsibilities. I also asked if you would help protect my credit rating by not reporting my account to the credit agencies as negative.

I have included the original letter and insert detailing the payment plan information. Please provide me with the name of the person I can contact in order to set up this arrangement. If you have any further questions regarding this matter, you can contact me at the numbers listed above.

Thank you for your cooperation.

Sincerely,

(Sign your name)

(Print your name)

YOU CAN'T MAKE THE MONTHLY PAYMENTS   *Follow-Up Letter 40*

Name / Date

Address 1

Address 2

Home and Work Phone

Social Security Number

On (Month/Day/Year) I sent a letter to your company explaining the reasons behind my having difficulties making my monthly payment and setting up a payment plan. I asked if you would respond within a month's time; however, a month has passed and I have not heard back from anyone regarding this matter.

Once again, I realize the importance, to both parties, of maintaining a good credit rating.

Knowing this, I have asked for your help in setting up a payment plan and taking my account out of collection, so that I may fulfill my responsibilities. I also asked if you would help protect my credit rating by not reporting my account to the credit agencies as negative.

I have included the original letter and insert detailing the payment plan information. Please provide me with the name of the person I can contact in order to set up this arrangement. If you have any further questions regarding this matter, you can contact me at the numbers listed above.

Thank you for your cooperation.

Sincerely,

(Sign your name)

(Print your name)

THIS ACCOUNT DOES NOT BELONG TO ME   *Follow-Up Letter 41*

Name / Date
Address 1
Address 2
Home and Work Phone
Social Security Number

On (Month/Day/Year) I sent a letter to your agency requesting the investigation and removal of inaccurate account information from my credit report. I asked if you would respond within a month's time; however, a month has passed and I have not heard back from anyone regarding this matter.

Once again, please investigate the accounts listed on the enclosed insert(s), under the provisions of the Fair Credit Reporting Act, 15 USC section 1681i. If the information I requested to be investigated is found to be inaccurate, all items that fall under this investigation must be removed immediately from my credit report and file.

Also, 15 USC sections 1681i(d) and 1681j of the Fair Credit Reporting Act require that I receive written notification of the updates, an up-to-date credit report (at no charge), and that an up-to-date credit report be sent to anyone who received my credit report within the last six months.

If you are having any difficulties completing this task, please contact me using the above information.

Thank you for your cooperation.

Sincerely,

(Sign your name)

(Print your name)

ACCOUNT IS TOO OLD

Follow-Up Letter 42

Name / Date
Address 1
Address 2
Home and Work Phone
Social Security Number

On (Month/Day/Year) I sent a letter to your agency requesting the investigation and removal of outdated account information posted to my credit report; however, my request has gone unanswered.

My original letter stated that a 30-day time period would constitute "reasonable time" for the removal of the outdated account information from my credit report, as mandated by the Fair Credit Reporting Act.

Once again, I realize the importance, to both parties, of having an accurate credit report. Knowing this, please investigate and remove the outdated account information listed on the enclosed insert from my credit report and file.

Also, 15 USC sections 1681i(d) and 1681j of the Fair Credit Reporting Act require that I receive written notification of the deletions, an up-to-date credit report (at no charge), and that an up-to-date credit report be sent to anyone who received my credit report within the last six months.

Thank you for your cooperation.

Sincerely,

(Sign your name)

(Print your name)

INQUIRY IS TOO OLD

Follow-Up Letter 43

Name / Date
Address 1
Address 2
Home and Work Phone
Social Security Number

On (Month/Day/Year) I sent a letter to your agency requesting the investigation and removal of outdated inquiry information posted to my credit report; however, my request has gone unanswered.

My original letter stated that a 30-day time period would constitute "reasonable time" for the removal of the outdated inquiry information from my credit report, as mandated by the Fair Credit Reporting Act.

Once again, I realize the importance, to both parties, of having an accurate credit report. Knowing this, please investigate and remove the outdated inquiry information listed on the enclosed insert from my credit report and file.

Also, 15 USC sections 1681i(d) and 1681j of the Fair Credit Reporting Act require that I receive written notification of the deletions, an up-to-date credit report (at no charge), and that an up-to-date credit report be sent to anyone who received my credit report within the last six months.

Thank you for your cooperation.

Sincerely,

(Sign your name)

(Print your name)

CONSUMER STATEMENT IS OLD

Follow-Up Letter 44

Name / Date
Address 1
Address 2
Home and Work Phone
Social Security Number

On (Month/Day/Year) I sent a letter to your agency requesting the investigation and removal of outdated consumer statement information posted to my credit report; however, my request has gone unanswered.

My original letter stated that a 30-day time period would constitute "reasonable time" for the removal of the outdated consumer statement information from my credit report, as mandated by the Fair Credit Reporting Act.

Once again, I realize the importance, to both parties, of having an accurate credit report. Knowing this, please investigate and remove the outdated consumer statement information listed on the enclosed insert from my credit report and file.

Also, 15 USC sections 1681i(d) and 1681j of the Fair Credit Reporting Act require that I receive written notification of the deletions, an up-to-date credit report (at no charge), and that an up-to-date credit report be sent to anyone who received my credit report within the last six months.

Thank you for your cooperation.

Sincerely,

(Sign your name)

(Print your name)

ACCOUNT WILL BE PAID IN FULL, IF . . . *Follow-Up Letter 45*

Name / Date
Address 1
Address 2
Home and Work Phone
Social Security Number

On (Month/Day/Year) I sent a letter to your company after realizing that I currently have an account that is reporting as a negative on my credit report. Furthermore, the letter expressed my willingness to settle the account. I asked if you would respond within a month's time; however, a month has passed and I have not heard back from anyone regarding this matter.

Once again, I realize the importance, to both parties, of maintaining a good credit rating.

Knowing this, I have asked for your help in settling my account, so that I may fulfill my responsibilities. I also asked if you would help protect my credit rating by reporting my account to the credit agencies as a unverifiable.

I have included the original letter and insert detailing the settlement information. Please provide me with the name of the person I can contact in order to set up this arrangement. If you have any further questions regarding this matter, you can contact me through the information listed above.

Thank you for your cooperation.

Sincerely,

(Sign your name)

(Print your name)

ADDING A CONSUMER STATEMENT

Follow-Up Letter 46

Name / Date
Address 1
Address 2
Home and Work Phone
Social Security Number

On (Month/Day/Year) I sent a letter to your agency requesting that a consumer statement be added to my credit report. My original letter stated that a 30-day time period would constitute "reasonable time" for the addition of the consumer statement to my credit report; however, my request has gone unanswered.

Once again, I realize the importance, to both parties, of having a complete and accurate credit report. In accordance with the Fair Credit Reporting Act 15 USC, 1681i(b), please add the consumer statement information listed on the enclosed insert to my credit report and file.

Also, 15 USC sections 1681i(d) and 1681j of the Fair Credit Reporting Act require that I receive written notification of the updates, an up-to-date credit report (at no charge), and that an up-to-date credit report be sent to anyone who received my credit report within the last six months.

If you are having any difficulties completing this task, please contact me using the above information.

Thank you for your cooperation.

Sincerely,

(Sign your name)

(Print your name)

Final Follow-Up Letters

The easy reference chart below allows you to find at a glance the Final Follow-Up Letter you will be using.

Final Follow-Up Letter #	Description
47	Yearly Free Report
48	Applicable Fee
49	Denial of Credit
50	Denial of Employment
51	Denial of Insurance
52	Denial of Rental Housing
53	Unemployed Seeking Employment
54	Victim of Fraud
55	Public Assistance Recipient
56	Updating Information on Credit Report
57	Adding New Accounts to Credit Report
58	Making a Late Payment (one time)
59	Account Does Not Belong to Me (1)
60	You Can't Make the Monthly Payments (1)
61	You Can't Make the Monthly Payments (2)
62	Account Does Not Belong to Me (2)
63	Account Is Too Old
64	Inquiry Is Too Old
65	Consumer Statement Is Too Old
66	Account Will Be Paid In Full, If . . .
67	Adding a Consumer Statement

YEARLY FREE REPORT   *Final Follow-Up Letter 47*

Name / Date
Address 1
Address 2
Home and Work Phone
Social Security Number

On (Month/Day/Year) I sent a follow-up letter to your agency requesting a complimentary copy of my credit report.

I have, once again, waited a "reasonable time" period for my request; however, my request has gone unanswered.

State regulations and the Fair Credit Reporting Act of 1970 allow me to receive a complimentary copy of my credit report once a year, upon request, at no charge. If you do not respond immediately to this third and last request by (Month/Day/Year) I will have no other choice but to contact the FTC or a similar regulatory agency.

Please send a complete complimentary copy of my credit report to the address provided above. I have included all previous correspondence to assist you in expediting the process. If you are having any difficulties completing this task, please contact me using the contact information listed above.

Thank you for your cooperation.

Sincerely,

(Sign your name)

(Print your name)

APPLICABLE FEE   *Final Follow-Up Letter 48*

Name / Date
Address 1
Address 2
Home and Work Phone
Social Security Number

On (Month/Day/Year) I sent a follow-up letter and a check in the amount of $_____ to your agency requesting a copy of my credit report.

I have, once again, waited a "reasonable time" period for my request; however, my request has gone unanswered.

State regulations and the Fair Credit Reporting Act of 1970 allow me to receive a copy of my credit report, upon request, as frequently as I wish. If you do not respond immediately to this third and last request by (Month/Day/Year) I will have no other choice but to contact the FTC or a similar regulatory agency.

Please send a complete complimentary copy of my credit report to the address provided above. I have included all previous correspondence to assist you in expediting the process. If you are having any difficulties completing this task, please contact me using the contact information listed above.

Thank you for your cooperation.

Sincerely,

(Sign your name)

(Print your name)

DENIAL OF CREDIT

Final Follow-Up Letter 49

Name / Date
Address 1
Address 2
Home and Work Phone
Social Security Number

On (Month/Day/Year) I sent a follow-up letter to your agency requesting a complimentary copy of my credit report due to your agency's credit report being used in determining my denial of credit.

I have, once again, waited a "reasonable time" period for my request; however, my request has gone unanswered.

State regulations and the Fair Credit Reporting Act of 1970 allow me to receive a complimentary copy of my credit report, if denied credit, at no charge. If you do not respond immediately to this third and last request by (Month/Day/Year) I will have no other choice but to contact the FTC or a similar regulatory agency.

Please send a complete complimentary copy of my credit report to the address provided above. I have included all previous correspondence to assist you in expediting the process. If you are having any difficulties completing this task, please contact me using the contact information listed above.

Thank you for your cooperation.

Sincerely,

(Sign your name)

(Print your name)

DENIAL OF EMPLOYMENT *Final Follow-Up Letter 50*

Name / Date
Address 1
Address 2
Home and Work Phone
Social Security Number

On (Month/Day/Year) I sent a follow-up letter to your agency requesting a complimentary copy of my credit report due to your agency's credit report being used in determining my denial for employment.

I have, once again, waited a "reasonable time" period for my request; however, my request has gone unanswered.

State regulations and the Fair Credit Reporting Act of 1970 allow me to receive a complimentary copy of my credit report, if denied employment, at no charge. If you do not respond immediately to this third and last request by (Month/Day/Year) I will have no other choice but to contact the FTC or a similar regulatory agency.

Please send a complete complimentary copy of my credit report to the address provided above. I have included all previous correspondence to assist you in expediting the process. If you are having any difficulties completing this task, please contact me using the contact information listed above.

Thank you for your cooperation.

Sincerely,

(Sign your name)

(Print your name)

DENIAL OF INSURANCE   *Final Follow-Up Letter 51*

Name / Date
Address 1
Address 2
Home and Work Phone
Social Security Number

On (Month/Day/Year) I sent a follow-up letter to your agency requesting a complimentary copy of my credit report due to your agency's credit report being used in determining my denial for insurance.

I have, once again, waited a "reasonable time" period for my request; however, my request has gone unanswered.

State regulations and the Fair Credit Reporting Act of 1970 allow me to receive a complimentary copy of my credit report, if denied insurance, at no charge. If you do not respond immediately to this third and last request by (Month/Day/Year) I will have no other choice but to contact the FTC or a similar regulatory agency.

Please send a complete complimentary copy of my credit report to the address provided above. I have included all previous correspondence to assist you in expediting the process. If you are having any difficulties completing this task, please contact me using the contact information listed above.

Thank you for your cooperation.

Sincerely,

(Sign your name)

(Print your name)

DENIAL OF RENTAL HOUSING

Final Follow-Up Letter 52

Name / Date
Address 1
Address 2
Home and Work Phone
Social Security Number

On (Month/Day/Year) I sent a follow-up letter to your agency requesting a complimentary copy of my credit report due to your agency's credit report being used in determining my denial for rental housing.

I have, once again, waited a "reasonable time" period for my request; however, my request has gone unanswered.

State regulations and the Fair Credit Reporting Act of 1970 allow me to receive a complimentary copy of my credit report, if denied rental housing, at no charge. If you do not respond immediately to this third and last request by (Month/Day/Year) I will have no other choice but to contact the FTC or a similar regulatory agency.

Please send a complete complimentary copy of my credit report to the address provided above. I have included all previous correspondence to assist you in expediting the process. If you are having any difficulties completing this task, please contact me using the contact information listed above.

Thank you for your cooperation.

Sincerely,

(Sign your name)

(Print your name)

UNEMPLOYED, SEEKING EMPLOYMENT   *Final Follow-Up Letter 53*

Name / Date
Address 1
Address 2
Home and Work Phone
Social Security Number

On (Month/Day/Year) I sent a follow-up letter to your agency requesting a complimentary copy of my credit report due to my being unemployed and seeking employment in the next 60 days.

I have, once again, waited a "reasonable time" period for my request; however, my request has gone unanswered.

State regulations and the Fair Credit Reporting Act of 1970 allow me to receive a complimentary copy of my credit report, if I am unemployed and seeking employment in the next 60 days, at no cost to me. If you do not respond immediately to this third and last request by (Month/Day/Year) I will have no other choice but to contact the FTC or a similar regulatory agency.

Please send a complete complimentary copy of my credit report to the address provided above. I have included all previous correspondence to assist you in expediting the process. If you are having any difficulties completing this task, please contact me using the contact information listed above.

Thank you for your cooperation.

Sincerely,

(Sign your name)

(Print your name)

VICTIM OF FRAUD   *Final Follow-Up Letter 54*

Name / Date
Address 1
Address 2
Home and Work Phone
Social Security Number

On (Month/Day/Year) I sent a follow-up letter to your agency requesting a complimentary copy of my credit report due to my being a victim of fraud.

I have, once again, waited a "reasonable time" period for my request; however, my request has gone unanswered.

State regulations and the Fair Credit Reporting Act of 1970 allow me to receive a complimentary copy of my credit report, if I am a victim of fraud, at no cost to me. If you do not respond immediately to this third and last request by (Month/Day/Year) I will have no other choice but to contact the FTC or a similar regulatory agency.

Please send a complete complimentary copy of my credit report to the address provided above. I have included all previous correspondence to assist you in expediting the process. If you are having any difficulties completing this task, please contact me using the contact information listed above.

Thank you for your cooperation.

Sincerely,

(Sign your name)

(Print your name)

PUBLIC ASSISTANCE RECIPIENT   *Final Follow-Up Letter 55*

Name / Date
Address 1
Address 2
Home and Work Phone
Social Security Number

On (Month/Day/Year) I sent a follow-up letter to your agency requesting a complimentary copy of my credit report due to my being a public assistance recipient.

I have, once again, waited a "reasonable time" period for my request; however, my request has gone unanswered.

State regulations and the Fair Credit Reporting Act of 1970 allow me to receive a complimentary copy of my credit report, if I am a public assistance recipient, at no cost to me. If you do not respond immediately to this third and last request by (Month/Day/Year) I will have no other choice but to contact the FTC or a similar regulatory agency.

Please send a complete complimentary copy of my credit report to the address provided above. I have included all previous correspondence to assist you in expediting the process. If you are having any difficulties completing this task, please contact me using the contact information listed above.

Thank you for your cooperation.

Sincerely,

(Sign your name)

(Print your name)

UPDATING INFORMATION ON CREDIT REPORT *Final Follow-Up Letter 56*

Name / Date
Address 1
Address 2
Home and Work Phone
Social Security Number

On (Month/Day/Year) I sent a follow-up letter to your agency requesting that information posted to my credit report be updated; however, as of (Month/Day/Year) my request has gone unanswered.

My original letter stated that a 30-day time period would constitute "reasonable time" for the updating of my credit report, as mandated by the Fair Credit Reporting Act. If you do not respond immediately to this third and last request by (Month/Day/Year) I will have no other choice but to contact the FTC or a similar regulatory agency.

Once again, I realize the importance, to both parties, of having an accurate credit report. Knowing this, please investigate and bring the information listed on the enclosed insert up to date on my credit report and file. Included is all previous correspondence to assist you.

Also, 15 USC sections 1681i(d) and 1681j of the Fair Credit Reporting Act require that I receive written notification of the updates, an up-to-date credit report (at no charge), and that an up-to-date credit report be sent to anyone who received my credit report within the last six months.

Thank you for your cooperation.

Sincerely,

(Sign your name)

(Print your name)

ADDING NEW ACCOUNTS TO CREDIT REPORT   *Final Follow-Up Letter 57*

Name / Date
Address 1
Address 2
Home and Work Phone
Social Security Number

On (Month/Day/Year) I sent a follow-up letter to your agency requesting that additional credit information be added to my credit report. However, as of (Month/Day/Year) my request has gone unanswered.

Once again, I realize the importance, to both parties, of maintaining up-to-date credit information. I know a great majority of your organization's success comes from providing individuals and businesses with the most complete and accurate credit report information. Knowing this, please investigate and add the credit information listed on the enclosed insert to my credit report and file.

My original letter stated that a 30-day time period would constitute "reasonable time" for the adding of these accounts to my credit report. If you do not respond immediately to this third and last request by (Month/Day/Year) I will have no other choice but to contact the FTC or a similar regulatory agency.

Also, 15 USC sections 1681i(d) and 1681j of the Fair Credit Reporting Act require that I receive written notification of the updates, an up-to-date credit report (at no charge), and that an up-to-date credit report be sent to anyone who received my credit report within the last six months. If you are having any difficulties completing this task, please contact me using the contact information listed above.

Thank you for your cooperation.

Sincerely,

(Sign your name)

(Print your name)

MAKING A LATE PAYMENT (ONE TIME) *Final Follow-Up Letter 58*

Name / Date
Address 1
Address 2
Home and Work Phone
Social Security Number

On (Month/Day/Year) I sent a follow-up letter to your company explaining the reasons behind my making a late payment. I asked if you would respond to my request within a month's time; however, as of (Month/Day/Year) I have not heard back from anyone regarding this matter.

I am including copies of my first two letters with this letter.

I realize the importance, to both parties, of maintaining a good credit rating. Knowing this, I, once again, ask for your help in protecting my credit rating by not reporting my account to the credit agencies as negative.

Please provide me with the name of the person I can contact in order to set up this arrangement. If you have any further questions regarding this matter, please contact me using the contact information listed above.

Thank you for your cooperation.

Sincerely,

(Sign your name)

(Print your name)

ACCOUNT DOES NOT BELONG TO ME   *Final Follow-Up Letter 59*

Name / Date
Address 1
Address 2
Home and Work Phone
Social Security Number

On (Month/Day/Year) I sent a follow-up letter to your agency requesting the investigation and removal of inaccurate account information from my credit report. I asked if you would respond to my requests within a month's time; however, as of (Month/Day/Year) I have not heard back from anyone regarding this matter.

I realize the importance, to both parties, of maintaining up-to-date credit information. I know a great majority of your organization's success comes from providing individuals and businesses with the most complete and accurate credit report information. Knowing this, please investigate the accounts listed on the enclosed insert(s), under the provisions of the Fair Credit Reporting Act, 15 USC section 1681i. If the information I requested to be investigated is found to be inaccurate, all items that fall under this investigation must be removed immediately from my credit report and file. If you do not respond immediately to this third and last request by (Month/Day/Year) I will have no other choice but to contact the FTC or a similar regulatory agency.

In order to help aid you in your investigation, I have been in contact with Mr./Mrs. _____, from (Name of Company), the person who is in charge of this matter. Mr./Mrs._____ can be contacted at (000) 000-0000.

Also, 15 USC sections 1681i(d) and 1681j of the Fair Credit Reporting Act require that I receive written notification of the updates, an up-to-date credit report (at no charge), and that an up-to-date credit report be sent to anyone who received my credit report within the last six months. If you are having any difficulties completing this task, please contact me using the contact information listed above.

Thank you for your cooperation.

Sincerely,

(Sign your name)

(Print your name)

YOU CAN'T MAKE THE MONTHLY PAYMENTS   *Final Follow-Up Letter 60*

Name / Date
Address 1
Address 2
Home and Work Phone
Social Security Number

On (Month/Day/Year) I sent a follow-up letter to your company explaining the reasons behind my having difficulties making my monthly payment and setting up a payment plan. I asked if you would respond to my requests within a month's time; however, as of (Month/Day/Year) I have not heard back from anyone regarding this matter.

I realize the importance, to both parties, of maintaining a good credit rating. Knowing this, I once again ask for your help in setting up a payment plan so that I may fulfill my responsibilities. I also ask if you would help protect my credit rating by not reporting my account to the credit agencies as negative.

I have included the original letter and insert detailing the payment plan information. Please provide me with the name of the person I can contact in order to set up this arrangement. If you have any further questions regarding this matter, please contact me using the contact information listed above.

Thank you for your cooperation.

Sincerely,

(Sign your name)

(Print your name)

YOU CAN'T MAKE THE MONTHLY PAYMENTS   *Final Follow-Up Letter 61*

Name / Date

Address 1

Address 2

Home and Work Phone

Social Security Number

On (Month/Day/Year) I sent a follow-up letter to your company explaining the reasons behind my having difficulties making my monthly payment and setting up a payment plan. I asked if you would respond to my requests within a month's time; however, as of (Month/Day/Year) I have not heard back from anyone regarding this matter.

I realize the importance, to both parties, of maintaining a good credit rating. Knowing this, I once again ask for your help in setting up a payment plan and taking my account out of collection so that I may fulfill my responsibilities. I also ask if you would help protect my credit rating by not reporting my account to the credit agencies as negative.

I have included the original letter and insert detailing the payment plan information. Please provide me with the name of the person I can contact in order to set up this arrangement. If you have any further questions regarding this matter, please contact me using the contact information listed above.

Thank you for your cooperation.

Sincerely,

(Sign your name)

(Print your name)

ACCOUNT DOES NOT BELONG TO ME   *Final Follow-Up Letter 62*

Name / Date
Address 1
Address 2
Home and Work Phone
Social Security Number

On (Month/Day/Year) I sent a follow-up letter to your agency requesting the investigation and removal of inaccurate account information from my credit report. I asked if you would respond to my requests within a month's time; however, as of (Month/Day/Year) I have not heard back from anyone regarding this matter.

I realize the importance, to both parties, of maintaining up-to-date credit information. I know a great majority of your organization's success comes from providing individuals and businesses with the most complete and accurate credit report information. Knowing this, please investigate the accounts listed on the enclosed insert(s), under the provisions of the Fair Credit Reporting Act, 15 USC section 1681i. If the information I requested to be investigated is found to be inaccurate, all items that fall under this investigation must be removed immediately from my credit report and file. If you do not respond immediately to this third and last request by (Month/Day/Year) I will have no other choice but to contact the FTC or a similar regulatory agency.

Also, 15 USC sections 1681i(d) and 1681j of the Fair Credit Reporting Act require that I receive written notification of the updates, an up-to-date credit report (at no charge), and that an up-to-date credit report be sent to anyone who received my credit report within the last six months. If you are having any difficulties completing this task, please contact me using the contact information listed above.

Thank you for your cooperation.

Sincerely,

(Sign your name)

(Print your name)

ACCOUNT IS TOO OLD   *Final Follow-Up Letter 63*

Name / Date
Address 1
Address 2
Home and Work Phone
Social Security Number

On (Month/Day/Year) I sent a follow-up letter to your agency requesting the investigation and removal of outdated account information posted to my credit report; however, as of (Month/Day/ Year) my request has gone unanswered.

My original letter stated that a 30-day time period would constitute "reasonable time" for the removal of outdated account information from my credit report, as mandated by the Fair Credit Reporting Act. If you do not respond immediately to this third and last request by (Month/Day/Year) I will have no other choice but to contact the FTC or a similar regulatory agency.

Once again, I realize the importance, to both parties, of having an accurate credit report. Knowing this, please investigate and remove the outdated account information listed on the enclosed insert from my credit report and file. Included is all previous correspondence to assist you.

Also, 15 USC sections 1681i(d) and 1681j of the Fair Credit Reporting Act require that I receive written notification of the deletions, an up-to-date credit report (at no charge), and that an up-to-date credit report be sent to anyone who received my credit report within the last six months.

Thank you for your cooperation.

Sincerely,

(Sign your name)

(Print your name)

INQUIRY IS TOO OLD *Final Follow-Up Letter 64*

Name / Date
Address 1
Address 2
Home and Work Phone
Social Security Number

On (Month/Day/Year) I sent a follow-up letter to your agency requesting the investigation and removal of outdated inquiry information posted to my credit report; however, as of (Month/Day/Year) my request has gone unanswered.

My original letter stated that a 30-day time period would constitute "reasonable time" for the removal of outdated inquiry information from my credit report, as mandated by the Fair Credit Reporting Act. If you do not respond immediately to this third and last request by (Month/Day/Year) I will have no other choice but to contact the FTC or a similar regulatory agency.

Once again, I realize the importance, to both parties, of having an accurate credit report. Knowing this, please investigate and remove the outdated inquiry information listed on the enclosed insert from my credit report and file. Included is all previous correspondence to assist you.

Also, 15 USC sections 1681i(d) and 1681j of the Fair Credit Reporting Act require that I receive written notification of the deletions, an up-to-date credit report (at no charge), and that an up-to-date credit report be sent to anyone who received my credit report within the last six months.

Thank you for your cooperation.

Sincerely,

(Sign your name)

(Print your name)

CONSUMER STATEMENT IS TOO OLD   *Final Follow-Up Letter 65*

Name / Date
Address 1
Address 2
Home and Work Phone
Social Security Number

On (Month/Day/Year) I sent a follow-up letter to your agency requesting the investigation and removal of outdated consumer statement information posted to my credit report; however, as of (Month/Day/Year) my request has gone unanswered.

My original letter stated that a 30-day time period would constitute "reasonable time" for the removal of outdated information from my credit report, as mandated by the Fair Credit Reporting Act. If you do not respond immediately to this third and last request by (Month/Day/Year) I will have no other choice but to contact the FTC or a similar regulatory agency.

Once again, I realize the importance, to both parties, of having an accurate credit report. Knowing this, please investigate and remove the outdated account information listed on the enclosed insert from my credit report and file. Included is all previous correspondence to assist you.

Also, 15 USC sections 1681i(d) and 1681j of the Fair Credit Reporting Act require that I receive written notification of the deletions, an up-to-date credit report (at no charge), and that an up-to-date credit report be sent to anyone who received my credit report within the last six months.

Thank you for your cooperation.

Sincerely,

(Sign your name)

(Print your name)

ACCOUNT WILL BE PAID IN FULL, IF . . . *Final Follow-Up Letter 66*

Name / Date
Address 1
Address 2
Home and Work Phone
Social Security Number

On (Month/Day/Year) I sent a follow-up letter to your company after realizing that I currently have an account that is reporting as a negative on my credit report. Furthermore, the letter expressed my willingness to settle the account. I asked if you would respond within a month's time; however, as of (Month/Day/Year) I have not heard back from anyone regarding this matter.

I realize the importance, to both parties, of maintaining a good credit rating. Knowing this, I, once again, ask for your help in settling my account so that I may fulfill my responsibilities. I also ask if you would help protect my credit rating by reporting my account to the credit agencies as a unverifiable.

I have included the original letter and insert detailing the settlement information. Please provide me with the name of the person I can contact in order to set up this arrangement. If you have any further questions regarding this matter, you can contact me through the information listed above.

Thank you for your cooperation.

Sincerely,

(Sign your name)

(Print your name)

ADDING A CONSUMER STATEMENT   *Final Follow-Up Letter 67*

Name / Date

Address 1

Address 2

Home and Work Phone

Social Security Number

On (Month/Day/Year) I sent a follow-up letter to your agency requesting that a consumer statement be added to my credit report; however, as of (Month/Day/Year) my request has gone unanswered.

My original letter stated that a 30-day time period would constitute "reasonable time" for the addition of the consumer statement to my credit report, as mandated by the Fair Credit Reporting Act. If you do not respond immediately to this third and last request by (Month/Day/Year) I will have no other choice but to contact the FTC or a similar regulatory agency.

I realize the importance, to both parties, of having a complete and accurate credit report. In accordance with the Fair Credit Reporting Act 15 USC, 1681i(b), please add the consumer statement information listed on the enclosed insert to my credit report and file.

Also, 15 USC sections 1681i(d) and 1681j of the Fair Credit Reporting Act require that I receive written notification of the updates, an up-to-date credit report (at no charge), and that an up-to-date credit report be sent to anyone who received my credit report within the last six months. If you are having any difficulties completing this task, please contact me using the above information.

Thank you for your cooperation.

Sincerely,

(Sign your name)

(Print your name)

Inserts

The easy reference chart below allows you to find at a glance the insert(s) you will need. Please refer to page 4 on how to use the inserts.

Insert Letter	Description
A	Original Goals
B	Questions You Should Ask
C	Revised Goals
D	Update Account on My Trans-Union Credit Report
E	Update Account on My Equifax Credit Report
F	Update Account on My Experian Credit Report
G	Add Account to My Credit Report
H	Change My Credit Report
I	Payment Plan Worksheet
J	Delete Account from My Credit Report
K	Delete Old Account from My Credit Report
L	Delete Old Inquiry from My Credit Report
M	Delete Old Consumer Statement from My Credit Report
N	Delete Account from My Credit Report

ORIGINAL GOALS   *(Insert A)*

In order to have a chance at successfully strengthening your credit rating, you need to set goals. Write out your goals in the spaces provided below. Remember, your original goals should be general, reachable, measurable, and time sensitive. The more general you keep your goals in the beginning, the easier they will be to revise.

GOAL 1: _____

_____

GOAL 2: _____

_____

GOAL 3: _____

_____

GOAL 4: _____

_____

GOAL 5: _____

_____

GOAL 6: _____

_____

GOAL 7: _____

_____

GOAL 8: _____

_____

GOAL 9: _____

_____

QUESTIONS YOU SHOULD ASK   *(Insert B)*

1. Company Name:

2. Company Address:

3. Name & Title of Company Representative:

4. What services does your company offer:

5. How long has your company been in business:

6. What will I be charged for:

7. Do you have a contract:

8. Can I get a copy of your contract to look over before I sign:

9. What guarantees does your company offer:

10. Does your company offer a Secured Credit Card:

11. What is the name of the company backing your card:

12. What charges apply to your card:

    Application Fees:

    Annual Fees:

    Finance Charges:

    Others:

13. What is the interest rate for your card:

14. Can I use your card to purchase any item or just certain items:

15. What is my line of credit based on:

16. Do you report to a credit agency as a regular account:

REVISED GOALS   *(Insert C)*

In order to have a chance at successfully strengthening your credit rating, you need to revise your original goals. Write out your goals in the spaces provided below. Remember, your revised goals should be specific, reachable, measurable, and time sensitive. The more specific your revised goals are the better your understanding will be of what needs to be fixed.

GOAL 1: _____

_____

GOAL 2: _____

_____

GOAL 3: _____

_____

GOAL 4: _____

_____

GOAL 5: _____

_____

GOAL 6: _____

_____

GOAL 7: _____

_____

GOAL 8: _____

_____

GOAL 9: _____

_____

UPDATE ACCOUNT ON MY CREDIT REPORT   *(Insert D)*

Full Name	
Social Security Number	
Date of Birth	
Home Address	

Please Update the Following Areas of My Trans-Union Credit Report with the Correct Information — (Page 1)

Correct General Information

☐ **Name:**
☐ **Social Security #:**
☐ **Date of Birth:**
☐ **Current Residency:**
☐ **Telephone Number:**
☐ **Former Residency:**
☐ **Current Employer:**
☐ **Former Employer:**

Correct Public Record Information

☐ **Court Type:**
☐ **Date Opened:**
☐ **Liabilities Involved:**
☐ **Type of Record:**
☐ **Assets Involved:**
☐ **Paid or Unpaid:**
☐ **Docket Number:**
☐ **Plaintiff/Attorney:**

UPDATE ACCOUNT ON MY CREDIT REPORT

(Insert D - cont.)

Full Name	
Social Security Number	
Date of Birth	
Home Address	

Please Update the Following Areas of My Trans-Union Credit Report with the Correct Information — (Page 2)

Correct Account Information

- ☐ Name of Business:
- ☐ Date Acct. Opened:
- ☐ High Credit:
- ☐ Current Balance:
- ☐ Amount Delinquent:
- ☐ Type of Account:
- ☐ Account Number:
- ☐ Term:
- ☐ Date Acct. Closed:
- ☐ ECOA Type:
- ☐ Loan Description:
- ☐ Payment History:

Correct Inquiries Information

- ☐ Date of Inquiry:
- ☐ ECOA Type:
- ☐ Name of Business:

Correct Consumer Statement Information

- ☐ Consumer Statement:

UPDATE ACCOUNT ON MY CREDIT REPORT   *(Insert E)*

Full Name	
Social Security Number	
Date of Birth	
Home Address	

Please Update the Following Areas of My Equifax Credit Report with the Correct Information — (Page 1)

Personal Identification Information

☐ Name:

☐ Current Residency:

☐ Former Residency:

☐ Social Security #:

☐ Date of Birth:

☐ Current Employer:

Correct Public Record Information

☐ Type of Record: ☐ Paid/Unpaid:

☐ Date Opened: ☐ Amount Owed:

☐ City of Origin: ☐ Date Released:

☐ Case/ID Number:

☐ Liabilities Involved:

☐ Assets Involved:

☐ Items Exempt:

☐ Type of Bankruptcy:

☐ Bankruptcy Filed:

☐ Bankruptcy Status:

☐ Plaintiff/Attorney:

☐ Amount Requested:

UPDATE ACCOUNT ON MY CREDIT REPORT   *(Insert E - cont.)*

Full Name	
Social Security Number	
Date of Birth	
Home Address	

Please Update the Following Areas of My Equifax Credit Report with the Correct Information — (Page 2)

Correct Collection Agency Account Information

☐ **Name of Agency:**

☐ **Phone Number:**

☐ **Date Reported:**

☐ **Creditors Name:**

☐ **Account Number:**

☐ **ECOA Account Type:**

☐ **Amount Owed:**

☐ **Account Balance:**

☐ **Account Status:**

☐ **Last Activity:**

Correct Credit Account Information

☐ **Name of Business:**

☐ **Account Number:**

☐ **ECOA Account Type:**

☐ **Date Acct. Opened:**

☐ **Type of Account:**

☐ **Account Status:**

☐ **High Credit:**

☐ **Account Terms:**

☐ **Account Balance:**

UPDATE ACCOUNT ON MY CREDIT REPORT   *(Insert E - cont.)*

Full Name	
Social Security Number	
Date of Birth	
Home Address	

Please Update the Following Areas of My Equifax Credit Report with the Correct Information — (Page 3)

Correct Credit Account Information (Cont'd)

☐ **Amount Past Due:**

☐ **Paying History:**

Correct Additional Information

☐ **Additional Info:**

Correct Companies That Requested Your Credit File Information

☐ **Date Requested:**

☐ **Name of Business:**

UPDATE ACCOUNT ON MY CREDIT REPORT   *(Insert F)*

Full Name	

Social Security Number	

Date of Birth	

Home Address	

Please Update the Following Areas of My Experian Credit Report with the Correct Information — (Page 1)

Correct Explanatory Information

☐   **Name:**

☐   **Current Residency:**

Correct Credit History (Public Record) Information

☐   **Court:**

☐   **Court Address:**

☐   **Docket/Cert. #:**

☐   **Type of Bankruptcy:**

☐   **Bankruptcy Status:**

☐   **Date Petitioned:**

☐   **Recorded Assets:**

☐   **Liabilities Involved:**

☐   **Responsibility:**

☐   **Civil Judgment Type:**

☐   **Civil Judgment Status:**

☐   **C.J. Filing Date:**

☐   **C.J. Amount:**

☐   **Plaintiff:**

☐   **Lien Type:**

☐   **Lien Amount:**

UPDATE ACCOUNT ON MY CREDIT REPORT   *(Insert F - cont.)*

Full Name	
Social Security Number	
Date of Birth	
Home Address	

Please Update the Following Areas of My Experian Credit Report with the Correct Information — (Page 2)

Correct Credit History (Account History) Information

☐ **Name of Account:** _____

☐ **Address of Account:** _____

☐ **Type of Business:** _____

☐ **Account Number:** _____

☐ **Type of Credit:** _____

☐ **Account Status:** _____

☐ **Date Opened:** _____

☐ **Account Terms:** _____

☐ **Responsibility:** _____

☐ **ECOA Acct. Type:** _____

☐ **Original Balance** _____

☐ **Account Status:** _____

☐ **Past Due:** _____

☐ **Delinquency:** _____

☐ **Account Balance:** _____

UPDATE ACCOUNT ON MY CREDIT REPORT   *(Insert F - cont.)*

Full Name	
Social Security Number	
Date of Birth	
Home Address	

Please Update the Following Areas of My Experian Credit Report with the Correct Information — (Page 3)

Correct Your Credit History Was Reviewed By Information

- ☐ **Name of Business:**
- ☐ **Address of Business:**
- ☐ **Type of Business:**
- ☐ **Date Rpt. Obtained:**
- ☐ **Reason for Report:**

Correct Please Help Us Help You Information

- ☐ **Name:**
- ☐ **Current Address:**
- ☐ **Former Addresses:**
- ☐ **Social Security #:**
- ☐ **Date of Birth:**
- ☐ **Spouse's Name:**

Correct Identification Information

- ☐ **Social Security #:**
- ☐ **Driver's License #:**
- ☐ **All Addresses:**
- ☐ **All Phone Numbers:**
- ☐ **All Employers:**

UPDATE ACCOUNT ON MY CREDIT REPORT   *(Insert F - cont.)*

Full Name	
Social Security Number	
Date of Birth	
Home Address	

Please Update the Following Areas of My Experian Credit Report with the Correct Information — (Page 4)

Correct Identification Information(Cont'd)

☐   **Other** _____

☐   **Date of Birth:** _____

☐   **Name:** _____

☐   **Rent or Own:** _____

☐   **Spouse's Name:** _____

☐   **Address Reported:** _____

☐   **Social Security #:** _____

ADD ACCOUNT TO MY CREDIT REPORT   *(Insert G)*

Full Name	
Social Security Number	
Date of Birth	
Home Address	

Please ADD the Following Account to My Credit Report:

☐   **Name of Company:**

☐   **Company Address:**

☐   **(City/State/Zip)**

☐   **Company's Phone Number:**

☐   **Type of Account:**

☐   **Account Number:**

☐   **Date Account Was Opened:**

☐   **Date of Last Payment:**

Your Signature:

CHANGE MY CREDIT REPORT   *(Insert H)*

Full Name	
Social Security Number	
Date of Birth	
Home Address	

Please CHANGE the Following Account Information on My Credit Report:

Correct Account Information

- ☐ **Name of Company:**
- ☐ **Company Address:**
- ☐ **(City/State/Zip)**
- ☐ **Company's Phone Number:**
- ☐ **Type of Account:**
- ☐ **Account Number:**
- ☐ **Date Account Was Opened:**
- ☐ **Date of Last Payment:**

Company Representative Signature:

Your Signature:

PAYMENT PLAN WORKSHEET   *(Insert I)*

Full Name	
Social Security Number	
Date of Birth	
Home Address	

The following information details a payment plan which I would be able to handle, in order to fulfill my responsibilities to your company.

Background Information

☐ **Name(s) on the Account:**

☐ **Account Number:**   **Amount Due:**

☐ **Credit Agency the Information Came From:**

☐ **Date Account Was Opened:**   **Date of Last Payment:**

☐ **Reason(s) Why the Payments Are Delinquent:**

Payment Plan Information

☐ **Payment Plan Start Date:**

☐ **Amount to Be Paid:** $ **(Weekly/Bi-Weekly)**

☐ **Payment Plan End Date:**

If this payment plan is acceptable, please sign and return this document to the address listed on the accompanying letter.

Company Representative Signature:

Your Signature:

DELETE ACCOUNT FROM MY CREDIT REPORT   *(Insert J)*

Full Name |
Social Security Number |
Date of Birth |
Home Address |

Please DELETE the Following Account Information from My Credit Report: The following account was reported, in error, to my credit report.

☐ **Name of Company:** _____

☐ **Company Address:** _____

☐ **(City/State/Zip)** _____

☐ **Company's Phone Number:** _____

☐ **Type of Account:** _____

☐ **Account Number:** _____

☐ **Date Account Was Opened:** _____

☐ **Date of Last Payment:** _____

_____

Company Representative Signature:

_____

Your Signature:

DELETE OLD ACCOUNT FROM MY CREDIT REPORT

(Insert K)

Full Name	
Social Security Number	
Date of Birth	
Home Address	

Please DELETE the Following Out-Dated Account Information from My Credit Report:

☐   **Name of Company:**

☐   **Company Address:**

☐   **(City/State/Zip)**

☐   **Company's Phone Number:**

☐   **Type of Account:**

☐   **Account Number:**

☐   **Date Account Was Opened:**

☐   **Date of Last Payment:**

Your Signature:

DELETE OLD INQUIRY FROM MY CREDIT REPORT   *(Insert L)*

Full Name	
Social Security Number	
Date of Birth	
Home Address	

Please DELETE the Following Out-Dated Inquiry Information from My Credit Report:

☐   **Name of Company:**

☐   **Company Address:**

☐   **(City/State/Zip)**

☐   **Company's Phone Number:**

☐   **Type of Inquiry:**

☐   **Date of Inquiry:**

Your Signature:

DELETE OLD CONSUMER STATEMENT
FROM MY CREDIT REPORT

(Insert M)

Full Name	
Social Security Number	
Date of Birth	
Home Address	

Please DELETE the Following Out-Dated Consumer Statement
from My Credit Report:

_____

_____

_____

_____

_____

_____

_____

_____

Your Signature:

DELETE ACCOUNT FROM MY CREDIT REPORT   *(Insert N)*

Full Name	
Social Security Number	
Date of Birth	
Home Address	

Please DELETE the Following Account Information from My Credit Report: The following account does not belong to me, having been reported to my credit report in error.

☐ **Name of Company:** _____

☐ **Company Address:** _____

☐ **(City/State/Zip)** _____

☐ **Company's Phone Number:** _____

☐ **Type of Account:** _____

☐ **Account Number:** _____

☐ **Date Account Was Opened:** _____

_____

Company Representative Signature:

_____

Your Signature:

Note Pads

The easy reference chart below allows you to find, at a glance, the insert(s) you will need. Please refer to page 64 on how to use the Note Pad inserts.

Insert Letter	Description
	Trans-Union Note Pads
AA	General Information Note Pad
BB	Summary Line Note Pad
CC	Public Record Note Pad
DD	Account Information Note Pad
EE	List of Inquires Note Pad
FF	Consumer Statement Note Pad
	Equifax Note Pads
GG	Personal Identification Information Note Pad
HH	Public Record Information Note Pad
II	Collection Account Information Note Pad
JJ	Credit Account Information Note Pad
KK	Additional Information Note Pad
LL	Companies That Requested Your Credit File Note Pad
	Experian Note Pads
MM	Your Credit History (Public Records) Note Pad
NN	Your Credit History (Account History) Note Pad
OO	Your Credit History Was Reviewed By Note Pad
PP	Please Help Us Help You Note Pad
QQ	Identification Information Note Pad

Trans-Union Note Pads

GENERAL INFORMATION NOTE PAD

(Insert AA)

Full Name	
Social Security Number	
Date of Birth	

Place an "OK" in the Status column if the information from the General Information section of your credit report is correct. If there is information on your credit report that you determine to be incorrect or inaccurate, place the word "Review" in the Status column, followed by the reason for investigating in the Reason column. Once you have determined the reason for the investigation, place the correct information in the column labeled "Replace with the Following Information." It will be helpful if you have substantiating proof defending your reason for the investigation.

QUESTIONED "GENERAL INFO." INFORMATION	*General Information Section Page 1*		CORRECTED "GENERAL INFO." INFORMATION
Credit Report Category	Status 1. Okay 2. Review	Reason (Explain why the information is being questioned.)	Replace with the Following Information
Name (6)			
Social Security # (7)			
Date of Birth (8)			
Current Address (9)			
Time at Current Address (10)			
Telephone Number (11)			

GENERAL INFORMATION NOTE PAD *(Insert AA-cont.)*

Full Name |

Social Security Number |

Date of Birth |

QUESTIONED "GENERAL INFO." INFORMATION	*General Information Section Page 2*		CORRECTED "GENERAL INFO." INFORMATION
Credit Report Category	**Status** 1. Okay 2. Review	**Reason (Explain why the information is being questioned.)**	**Replace with the Following Information**
Former Address (12)			
Time at Former Address (10)			
Current Employer (13)			
Current Employer Address (13)			
Position (work) (14)			
Income (14)			
Time at Current Employer (15)			
Former Employer (16)			
Former Employer Address (16)			
Income (14)			
Time at Former Employer (15)			

SUMMARY LINE NOTE PAD   *(Insert BB)*

Full Name	
Social Security Number	
Date of Birth	

Place an "OK" in the Status column if the information from the Summary Line section of your credit report is correct. If there is information on your credit report that you determine to be incorrect or inaccurate, place the word "Review" in the Status column, followed by the reason for investigating in the Reason column. Once you have determined the reason for the investigation, place the correct information in the column labeled "Replace with the Following Information." It is helpful if you have substantiating proof defending your reason for the investigation.

Summary Line Section

QUESTIONED "SUMMARY LINE" INFORMATION				CORRECTED "SUMMARY LINE" INFORMATION
Credit Report Category	Status 1. Okay 2. Review	Reason (Explain why the information is being questioned.)		Replace with the Following Information
Number of Accounts (17)				
Number of Negative Accounts (18)				
Number of Accounts Turned Over to Collection (20)				
Number of Inquires (21)				
Current Balance of Open Accounts (22)				
High Credit/Credit Limit (23)				

PUBLIC RECORD NOTE PAD

(Insert CC)

Full Name	

Social Security Number	

Type of Public Record	

Docket Number	

Place an "OK" in the Status column if the information from the Public Record section of your credit report is correct. If there is information on your credit report that you determine to be incorrect or inaccurate, place the word "Review" in the Status column, followed by the reason for investigating in the Reason column. Once you have determined the reason for the investigation, place the correct information in the column labeled "Replace with the Following Information." It is helpful if you have substantiating proof defending your reason for the investigation.

QUESTIONED "PUBLIC RECORD" INFORMATION	*Public Record Section Page 1*		CORRECTED "PUBLIC RECORD" INFORMATION
Credit Report Category	Status 1. Okay 2. Review	Reason (Explain why the information is being questioned.)	Replace with the Following Information
Source Code (24)			
Type of Court (25)			
Date of Public Record (26)			
Amount of Liability (21)			
Type of Public Record (22)			
High Credit/Credit Limit (23)			

PUBLIC RECORD NOTE PAD

(Insert CC-cont.)

Full Name |

Social Security Number |

Type of Public Record |

Docket Number |

QUESTIONED "PUBLIC RECORD" INFORMATION	*Public Record Section Page 1*		CORRECTED "PUBLIC RECORD" INFORMATION

Credit Report Category	Status 1. Okay 2. Review	Reason (Explain why the information is being questioned.)	Replace with the Following Information
Amount of Assets (29)			
Public Record Open/ Closed (30)			
Docket Number (31)			
Plaintiff/Attorney (32)			

ACCOUNT INFORMATION NOTE PAD   *(Insert DD)*

Full Name	
Social Security Number	
Name of Account	
Account Number	

Place an "OK" in the Status column if the information from the Account Information section of your credit report is correct. If there is information on your credit report that you determine to be incorrect or inaccurate, place the word "Review" in the Status column, followed by the reason for investigating in the Reason column. Once you have determined the reason for the investigation, place the correct information in the column labeled "Replace with the Following Information." It is helpful if you have substantiating proof defending your reason for the investigation.

QUESTIONED "ACCOUNT INFO" INFORMATION	*Account Information / Trades Section Page 1*		CORRECTED "ACCOUNT INFO" INFORMATION
Credit Report Category	Status 1. Okay 2. Review	Reason (Explain why the information is being questioned.)	Replace with the Following Information
Sub. Name (33)			
Date Account Opened (38)			
Beginning Balance (39)			
Current Balance (42)			
Amount Delinquent (43)			
Account Number (34)			

ACCOUNT INFORMATION NOTE PAD   *(Insert DD-cont.)*

Full Name	

Social Security Number	

Name of Account	

Account Number	

QUESTIONED "ACCOUNT INFO" INFORMATION	*Account Information / Trades Section* *Page 2*		CORRECTED "ACCOUNT INFO" INFORMATION
Credit Report Category	Status 1. Okay 2. Review	Reason (Explain why the information is being questioned.)	Replace with the Following Information
Term of the Loan (37)			
Date Account Closed (41)			
ECOA Account Designator (47)			
Account Description (48)			
Number of Late Payments (45)			

LIST OF INQUIRIES NOTE PAD

(Insert EE)

Full Name	
Social Security Number	
Date of Birth	

Place an "OK" in the Status column if the information from the List of Inquiries Information section of your credit report is correct. If there is information on your credit report that you determine to be incorrect or inaccurate, place the word "Review" in the Status column, followed by the reason for investigating in the Reason column. Once you have determined the reason for the investigation, place the correct information in the column labeled "Replace with the Following Information." It is helpful if you have substantiating proof defending your reason for the investigation.

QUESTIONED "INQUIRY INFO" INFORMATION	*List of Inquiries Section*		CORRECTED "INQUIRY INFO" INFORMATION
Credit Report Category	Status 1. Okay 2. Review	Reason (Explain why the information is being questioned.)	Replace with the Following Information
Date of Inquiry (50)			
ECOA Account Designator (51)			
Subject Name (53)			

CONSUMER STATEMENT NOTE PAD

(Insert FF)

Full Name	

Social Security Number	

Date of Birth	

Place an "OK" in the Status column if the information from the Consumer Statement section of your credit report is correct. If there is information on your credit report that you determine to be incorrect or inaccurate, place the word "Review" in the Status column, followed by the reason for investigating in the Reason column. Once you have determined the reason for the investigation, place the correct consumer statement in the column labeled "Replace with the Following Information." Hopefully you have substantiating proof defending your reason for the investigation.

QUESTIONED "CONSUMER STATEMENT" INFORMATION

Consumer Statement Section

Credit Report Category	Status 1. Okay 2. Review	Reason (Explain why the information is being questioned.)
Consumer Statement (54)		

Correct Consumer Statement Information
Replace with the Following Consumer Statement (if any)

_____

_____

_____

_____

Equifax Note Pads

PERSONAL IDENTIFICATION INFORMATION NOTE PAD   *(Insert GG)*

Full Name	

Social Security Number	

Date of Birth	

Place an "OK" in the Status column if the information from the Personal Identification section of your credit report is correct. If there is information on your credit report that you determine to be incorrect or inaccurate, place the word "Review" in the Status column, followed by the reason for investigating in the Reason column. Once you have determined the reason for the investigation, place the correct information in the column labeled "Replace with the Following Information." It is helpful if you have substantiating proof defending your reason for the investigation.

QUESTIONED "PERSONAL ID" INFORMATION	*Personal Identification Section*		CORRECTED "PERSONAL ID" INFORMATION
Credit Report Category	Status 1. Okay 2. Review	Reason (Explain why the information is being questioned.)	Replace with the Following Information
Name (4)			
Current Address (5)			
Former Address (6)			
Social Security # (7)			
Last Reported Employer (10)			

PUBLIC RECORD INFORMATION NOTE PAD   *(Insert HH)*

Full Name	

Social Security Number	

Type of Public Record	

Case / ID Number	

Place an "OK" in the Status column if the information from the Public Record Information section of your credit report is correct. If there is information on your credit report that you determine to be incorrect or inaccurate, place the word "Review" in the Status column, followed by the reason for investigating in the Reason column. Once you have determined the reason for the investigation, place the correct information in the column labeled "Replace with the Following Information." It is helpful if you have substantiating proof defending your reason for the investigation.

QUESTIONED "PUBLIC RECORD" INFORMATION	*Public Record Information Section Page 1*		CORRECTED "PUBLIC RECORD" INFORMATION
Credit Report Category	Status 1. Okay 2. Review	Reason (Explain why the information is being questioned.)	Replace with the Following Information
Type of Public Record (10)			
Date of Public Record (11)			
Case/ID Number (13)			
Amount of Liability (14)			
Amount of Assets (15)			

PUBLIC RECORD INFORMATION NOTE PAD   *(Insert HH-cont.)*

> Full Name |

> Social Security Number |

> Type of Public Record |

> Case / ID Number |

QUESTIONED "PUBLIC RECORD" INFORMATION	*Public Record Information Section Page 2*		CORRECTED "PUBLIC RECORD" INFORMATION
Credit Report Category	Status 1. Okay 2. Review	Reason (Explain why the information is being questioned.)	Replace with the Following Information
Exempt (16)			
Type (Bankruptcy Only) (17)			
Filed (18)			
Status (19)			
Plaintiff/Attorney (20)			
Amount (21)			
(Un) Satisfied (22)			
Verified (23)			
Amount Owed (24)			
Date Released (25)			

COLLECTION ACCOUNT INFORMATION NOTE PAD   *(Insert II)*

Full Name	

Social Security Number	

Name of Creditor	

Account Number	

Place an "OK" in the Status column if the information from the Collection Agency Account Information section of your credit report is correct. If there is information on your credit report that you determine to be incorrect or inaccurate, place the word "Review" in the Status column, followed by the reason for investigating in the Reason column. Once you have determined the reason for the investigation, place the correct information in the column labeled "Replace with the Following Information." It is helpful if you have substantiating proof defending your reason for the investigation.

QUESTIONED "COLLECTION AGENCY" INFORMATION	*Collection Agency Account Information Section*		CORRECTED "COLLECTION AGENCY" INFORMATION
Credit Report Category	Status 1. Okay 2. Review	Reason (Explain why the information is being questioned.)	Replace with the Following Information
Creditor's Name (31)			
Account Number (32)			
ECOA Account Type Designator (33)			
Amount (34)			
Balance (35)			
Status (36)			

CREDIT ACCOUNT INFORMATION NOTE PAD

(Insert JJ)

Full Name	
Social Security Number	
Name of Account	
Account Number	

Place an "OK" in the Status column if the information from the Credit Account Information section of your credit report is correct. If there is information on your credit report that you determine to be incorrect or inaccurate, place the word "Review" in the Status column, followed by the reason for investigating in the Reason column. Once you have determined the reason for the investigation, place the correct information in the column labeled "Replace with the Following Information." It is helpful if you have substantiating proof defending your reason for the investigation.

QUESTIONED "ACCOUNT INFO" INFORMATION	*Credit Account Information Section Page 1*		CORRECTED "ACCOUNT INFO" INFORMATION
Credit Report Category	Status 1. Okay 2. Review	Reason (Explain why the information is being questioned.)	Replace with the Following Information
Company Name (38)			
Account Number (39)			
Whose Account (40)			
Date Opened (41)			
Type of Account (42)			
Status (44)			

CREDIT ACCOUNT INFORMATION NOTE PAD (Insert JJ-cont.)

Full Name |

Social Security Number |

Name of Account |

Account Number |

QUESTIONED "ACCOUNT INFO" INFORMATION	Credit Account Information Section Page 2		CORRECTED "ACCOUNT INFO" INFORMATION
Credit Report Category	Status 1. Okay 2. Review	Reason (Explain why the information is being questioned.)	Replace with the Following Information
High Credit (45)			
Terms (46)			
Balance (47)			
Past Due (48)			
Prior Paying History (51)			

ADDITIONAL INFORMATION NOTE PAD

(Insert KK)

Full Name	
Social Security Number	
Date of Birth	

When listing the items you wish investigated on your credit report from the Additional Information section, circle either "Remove" or "Update." If you choose "Remove," fill in the area labeled "Incorrect Information" with the information you wish to have removed. If you choose "Update," fill in the area labeled "Incorrect Information." If you are updating information, you also fill in the area labeled "Correct Information" with the information you feel to be correct. Use a separate statement for each entry you make.

Additional Information Section
Page 1

1. Please (**Remove/Update**) the following information located in the Additional Information section of my credit report:

   (**Incorrect Information**): _____

   _____

   (**Corrected Information**): _____

   _____

2. Please (**Remove/Update**) the following information located in the Additional Information section of my credit report:

   (**Incorrect Information**): _____

   _____

   (**Corrected Information**): _____

   _____

ADDITIONAL INFORMATION NOTE PAD   *(Insert KK-cont.)*

Full Name	

Social Security Number	

Date of Birth	

Additional Information Section
Page 2

3. Please **(Remove/Update)** the following information located in the Additional Information section of my credit report:

(Incorrect Information):
_____

(Corrected Information):
_____

4. Please **(Remove/Update)** the following information located in the Additional Information section of my credit report:

(Incorrect Information):
_____

(Corrected Information):
_____

5. Please **(Remove/Update)** the following information located in the Additional Information section of my credit report:

(Incorrect Information):
_____

(Corrected Information):
_____

COMPANIES THAT REQUESTED YOUR CREDIT FILE NOTE PAD *(Insert LL)*

Full Name	

Social Security Number	

Date of Birth	

Place an "OK" in the Status column if the information from the Companies That Requested Your Credit File section of your credit report is correct. If there is information on your credit report that you determine to be incorrect or inaccurate, place the word "Review" in the Status column, followed by the reason for investigating in the Reason column. Once you have determined the reason for the investigation, place the correct information in the column labeled "Replace with the Following Information." It is helpful if you have substantiating proof defending your reason for the investigation.

QUESTIONED "INQUIRY INFO" INFORMATION	*Companies That Requested Your Credit File Section*		CORRECTED "INQUIRY INFO" INFORMATION
Credit Report Category	Status 1. Okay 2. Review	Reason (Explain why the information is being questioned.)	Replace with the Following Information
Date (52)			
Business Name (53)			

Experian Note Pads

YOUR CREDIT HISTORY (PUBLIC RECORDS) NOTE PAD   *(Insert MM)*

Full Name	
Social Security Number	
Type of Public Record	
Docket / Cert. Number	

Place an "OK" in the Status column if the information from the Your Credit History section of your credit report is correct. If there is information on your credit report that you determine to be incorrect or inaccurate, place the word "Review" in the Status column, followed by the reason for investigating in the Reason column. Once you have determined the reason for the investigation, place the correct information in the column labeled "Replace with the Following Information." It is helpful if you have substantiating proof defending your reason for the investigation.

QUESTIONED "CREDIT HISTORY" INFORMATION	*Your Credit History Section (Public Records) Page 1*		CORRECTED "CREDIT HISTORY" INFORMATION
Credit Report Category	Status 1. Okay 2. Review	Reason (Explain why the information is being questioned.)	Replace with the Following Information
Court (6)			
Court Address (7)			
Docket/Certificate # (8)			
Bankruptcy Type (9)			
Bankruptcy Status (10)			
Petitioned (11)			

YOUR CREDIT HISTORY (PUBLIC RECORDS) NOTE PAD *(Insert MM-cont.)*

Full Name |

Social Security Number |

Type of Public Record |

Docket / Cert. Number |

QUESTIONED "CREDIT HISTORY" INFORMATION		*Your Credit History Section (Public Records) Page 2*	CORRECTED "CREDIT HISTORY" INFORMATION
Credit Report Category	Status 1. Okay 2. Review	Reason (Explain why the information is being questioned.)	Replace with the Following Information
Recorded Assets (12)			
Liabilities (13)			
Responsibility (14)			
Civil Judgment Type (15)			
Civil Judgment Status (16)			
Original Filing Date (17)			
Civil Judgment Amount (18)			
Plaintiff (19)			
Lien Type (20)			
Lien Amount (21)			

YOUR CREDIT HISTORY (ACCOUNT HISTORY) NOTE PAD   *(Insert NN)*

Full Name |

Social Security Number |

Name of Account |

Account Number |

Place an "OK" in the Status column if the information from the Your Credit History section of your credit report is correct. If there is information on your credit report that you determine to be incorrect or inaccurate, place the word "Review" in the Status column, followed by the reason for investigating in the Reason column. Once you have determined the reason for the investigation, place the correct information in the column labeled "Replace with the Following Information." It is helpful if you have substantiating proof defending your reason for the investigation.

QUESTIONED "ACCT. HISTORY" INFORMATION	*Your Credit History Section (Account History) Page 1*		CORRECTED "ACCT. HISTORY" INFORMATION
Credit Report Category	**Status** 1. Okay 2. Review	**Reason (Explain why the information is being questioned.)**	**Replace with the Following Information**
Name of Account (22)			
Address of Account (23)			
Account Number (25)			
Type of Credit (26)			
Date Opened (27)			
Term (28)			

YOUR CREDIT HISTORY (ACCOUNT HISTORY) NOTE PAD *(Insert NN-cont.)*

Full Name	

Social Security Number	

Name of Account	

Account Number	

QUESTIONED "ACCT. HISTORY" INFORMATION	*Your Credit History Section (Account History) Page 2*		CORRECTED "ACCT. HISTORY" INFORMATION
Credit Report Category	Status 1. Okay 2. Review	Reason (Explain why the information is being questioned.)	Replace with the Following Information
ECOA Account Type Designator (30)			
Original Amount (31)			
Account Status (33)			
Past Due (34)			
Delinquency (35)			
Payment History (37)			
Times Late (38)			
Balance History (39)			

YOUR CREDIT HISTORY WAS REVIEWED BY NOTE PAD   *(Insert OO)*

Full Name	
Social Security Number	
Date of Birth	

Place an "OK" in the Status column if the information from the Your Credit History Was Reviewed By section of your credit report is correct. If there is information on your credit report that you determine to be incorrect or inaccurate, place the word "Review" in the Status column, followed by the reason for investigating in the Reason column. Once you have determined the reason for the investigation, place the correct information in the column labeled "Replace with the Following Information." It is helpful if you have substantiating proof defending your reason for the investigation.

QUESTIONED "INQUIRY INFO" INFORMATION	*Your Credit History Was Reviewed By Section*		CORRECTED "INQUIRY INFO" INFORMATION
Credit Report Category	Status 1. Okay 2. Review	Reason (Explain why the information is being questioned.)	Replace with the Following Information
Name (41)			
Address (42)			
Business Type (43)			
Reason (45)			
Other (46)			

PLEASE HELP US HELP YOU NOTE PAD   *(Insert PP)*

Full Name	
Social Security Number	
Date of Birth	

Place an "OK" in the Status column if the information from the Please Help Us Help You section of your credit report is correct. If there is information on your credit report that you determine to be incorrect or inaccurate, place the word "Review" in the Status column, followed by the reason for investigating in the Reason column. Once you have determined the reason for the investigation, place the correct information in the column labeled "Replace with the Following Information." It is helpful if you have substantiating proof defending your reason for the investigation.

QUESTIONED "PLEASE HELP..." INFORMATION	*Please Help Us Help You Section*		CORRECTED "PLEASE HELP..." INFORMATION
Credit Report Category	Status 1. Okay 2. Review	Reason (Explain why the information is being questioned.)	Replace with the Following Information
Your Name (48)			
Address (49)			
Other Addresses (50)			
Social Security Number (51)			
Date of Birth (52)			
Spouse's Name (53)			

IDENTIFICATION INFORMATION NOTE PAD   *(Insert QQ)*

Full Name	

Social Security Number	

Date of Birth	

Place an "OK" in the Status column if the information from the Identification Information section of your credit report is correct. If there is information on your credit report that you determine to be incorrect or inaccurate, place the word "Review" in the Status column, followed by the reason for investigating in the Reason column. Once you have determined the reason for the investigation, place the correct information in the column labeled "Replace with the Following Information." It is helpful if you have substantiating proof defending your reason for the investigation.

Identification Information Section

QUESTIONED "ID INFO." INFORMATION			CORRECTED "ID INFO." INFORMATION
Credit Report Category	Status 1. Okay 2. Review	Reason (Explain why the information is being questioned.)	Replace with the Following Information
Social Security Number (54)			
Driver's License Number (55)			
Addresses (56)			
Type of Residence (57)			
Telephone Number(s) (58)			
Employers (59)			
Other (60)			

Glossary

Account An account is a record of information that is kept by a lender, business, or agency. The information in the account allows a lender, business, or agency to keep track of vital information, such as name, address, amount owed, monthly payment, and payment history.

Account (Bad) A bad account is one that appears on your credit report with negative information due to any number of reasons, such as late payments, missed payments, or no payments.

Account (Good) A good account is one that appears on your credit report with positive information, such as early payments, on-time payments, or payment in full.

Account Classification An account classification is a method used by credit agencies to identify what type of account the consumer opened.

Account Rating An account rating is a credit term that is determined by a variety of outside factors, such as credit worthiness, credit analysis, credit capacity, and credit stability.

Assets An asset is anything you have that holds monetary value, such as a boat, a car, cash, a home, land, jewelry, a business, or a life insurance policy.

Authorized User An authorized user is a person who has the right to use another person's account.

Bad Debt A bad debt is a debt that has not been satisfied according to the agreed-upon terms.

Bankruptcy Bankruptcy is a legal proceeding that declares a person or business insolvent, relieving them from paying back certain debts.

Bankruptcy (Chapter 7) A Chapter 7 bankruptcy is a legal proceeding that declares a person insolvent, relieving them from paying back creditors.

Bankruptcy (Chapter 13) A Chapter 13 bankruptcy is a legal proceeding that declares a person insolvent and sets up a payment plan determined by the court, after which the bankruptcy is discharged.

Certificate of Deposit A certificate of deposit is a "certificate from a bank stating that the named party has a specified sum on deposit . . . "

Charge-Off A charge-off is a credit term given to an account that a creditor was unable to collect and reported as a bad account.

Civil Judgment A civil judgment is a court order that legally forces a person to pay a certain amount of money.

Collection A collection is the credit term used when an account goes into default. The account is usually turned over to a collection agency.

Collection Agency A collection agency is a business whose job is to collect another business's unpaid accounts.

Consumer File A consumer file is a record of all the information collected and recorded by a consumer reporting agency.

Consumer Report / Credit Report A consumer report/credit report is a part of the consumer file on which select credit information is recorded; it may be requested for legitimate business purposes.

Consumer Reporting Agency, Credit Agency, or Credit Bureau A consumer reporting agency, credit agency, or credit bureau is "any person, for monetary fees, dues, or on a cooperative basis, who regularly engages in whole or part in the practice of assembling or evaluating consumer credit information or other information on consumers for the purposes of furnishing consumer reports to third parties, and which uses any means or facility of interstate commerce for the purpose of preparing or furnishing consumer reports."

Consumer Statement A consumer statement is a written statement of a 100 words or less that is added to the end of the credit report explaining any credit situation.

Cosigner A cosigner is a person who signs his or her name to another person's account, providing stability and assuming responsibility should the account default.

Cosigner (Primary) A primary cosigner is the first person who signs his or her name to an account, and who is primarily responsible for the account.

Cosigner (Shared) A shared cosigner is a person who signs his or her name to an account and shares equal responsibility for maintaining the account.

Credit Analysis A credit analysis is an evaluation process a credit grantor uses in order to determine a consumer's credit worthiness.

Credit Capacity Credit capacity is the amount of credit a consumer can handle according to their credit analysis.

Credit Grantor A credit grantor is an individual or business who extends a line of credit.

Credit History A credit history is a record of credit reported to the credit agency, beginning with the first time credit is used.

Credit Reference A credit reference is an individual or business with whom a credit account has been established.

Credit Stability Credit stability is one way of measuring credit worthiness, and is derived from doing a credit analysis. It is determined by such areas as credit history, debt-to-income ratio, time at job, and time at residency.

Credit Standing Credit standing is the current status of one's credit.

Credit Worthiness Credit worthiness is the strength of one's credit, which is determined by such factors as credit history, credit standing, employment history, debt-to-income ratio, residency, and income.

Creditor A creditor is a person or business who extends credit and to whom money is owed.

Debt A debt is money owed to someone else.

Debt-to-Income Ratio Debt-to-income ratio is the ratio of one's debts to the amount of one's income.

Defendant A defendant is a legal term given to a person who is taken to court by a plaintiff.

Discharge A discharge is a legal term used during a bankruptcy, releasing the debts owed to creditors.

Docket Number A docket number is an identification number assigned to a particular court case.

ECOA The ECOA is short for the "Equal Credit Opportunity Act." The ECOA is an act passed through legislation protecting both consumers and creditors from unfair credit practices. The ECOA prohibits discrimination on the basis of race, color, religion, nation of origin, sex, marital status, age, receipt of public assistance, or good faith exercise of any rights under the Consumer Credit Protection Act.

Equifax Equifax is one of the three major credit reporting agencies in the United States.

Experian Experian is one of the three major credit reporting agencies in the United States.

FCRA The FCRA is short for the "Fair Credit Reporting Act." The FCRA is a piece of legislation that regulates the processes of gathering and reporting credit information to credit files and credit reports.

Foreclosure A foreclosure is a legal proceeding giving a lender who has a lien on a real estate property the right to take possession of the property as a result of nonpayment or a breach of contract. The lender is also able to put the property up for sale in order to recover the unpaid debt.

Good Standing Good standing is a credit term given to an account that has been or is up to date and paid as agreed.

History of Payments (Historical Status) A history of payments, which is located in the account information section, is a record of monthly payments made on an account.

Interest Interest is the percentage a creditor charges on money borrowed, usually on the outstanding balance.

Liability Liability is the amount of debt one is responsible for.

Lien A lien is a notice posted to an asset by a creditor, telling the consumer and other creditors there is money owed.

Line of Credit A line of credit is an open-ended agreement that allows the user of the account the freedom to purchase without having to pay cash at the time of purchase.

Loan A loan is a financial transaction in which a lender allows a consumer to borrow money, giving the consumer a timetable by which the money must be paid back, usually with interest.

MOP MOP is short for "Manner of Payment." The MOP, one of the categories found on the credit report, lists the information known as the payment history.

Non-Verification Non-verification is a credit term used when a credit agency does not reply to an inquiry within the 30 days prescribed by the FCRA.

Plaintiff Plaintiff is a legal term given to a person who takes a defendant to court.

Primary User A primary user is the first signer on an account, who is primarily held responsible in the case of default.

Reasonable Time Reasonable time refers to a time limit on an investigation of credit, primarily for credit agencies, set up to ensure a prompt response.

Repossession A repossession is the action of taking back financed property, by a lender, due to a breach of contract such as late payments or nonpayment.

Shared Account A shared account is an account in which all signers to the account are equally responsible.

Statute A statute is a state law passed to protect the consumer.

Subscriber A subscriber is a term used by the credit agencies for those who are signed up to do business with the agencies.

Tax Lien A tax lien is a notice posted to your credit file and credit report stating you owe a certain amount of money to the government, both state and federal, for taxes that have gone unpaid.

Trans-Union Trans-Union is one of the three major credit reporting agencies in the United States.

Undesignated Account An undesignated account is an account that has no record of payment history.

References

American Heritage College Dictionary (1997) (third edition). New York: Houghton Mifflin Company.

Azzata, G., Esq. (1988). *Equal Credit Opportunity Act* (second edition). Boston: National Consumer Law Center Inc.

Better Business Bureau. [Online] Available *www.bbb.org.* 1998.

Cane, M.A. (1995). *The Five-Minute Lawyer's Guide to Bad Debts, Credit Problems, and Bankruptcy.* New York: Bantam Doubleday Dell Publishing Group, Inc.

CardLearn: Secured Cards. [Online] Available *www.ramresearch.com/cardlearn/ secured.html.* 1998.

CardTrak: CardTrak's Secured Card Survey. [Online] Available *www.ramresearch.com/cardtrak/survey.html.* February, 1998.

CCH Editorial Staff. (1994). *Consumer Credit Guide* (Vol. 6). Chicago: CCH, Inc.

Dunkin, Amy, ed. (1996). "The best moves if you're broke." *Business Week,* August 1996, Vol. 272:1, pp. 110-111.

Equifax. [Online] Available *www.equifax.com.* 1998.

Experian. [Online] Available *www.experian.com.* 1998.

Federal Trade Commission. [Online] Available *www.ftc.org.* 1997.

Finance Center: Secured Credit Cards. Available *www.financenter.com/cards.htm.* 1997.

Fonseca, John R., ed. (1985). *Handling Consumer Credit Cases.* (3rd. edition, Vol. 1). San Francisco: Baincroft-Whitney Co.

Green, Ella, ed. (1995). 1996 *Consumer's Resource Handbook.* Washington, D.C.: United States Office of Consumer Affairs.

Hale, Roger H. (1983). *Credit Analysis: A Complete Guide.* New York: John Wiley & Sons, Inc.

Hausker, A.J. (1991). *Fundamentals of Public Credit Analysis.* London: Jai Press, Inc.

Keest, K.E. (1995). *The Cost of Credit: Regulation and Legal Challenges.* Boston: National Consumer Law Center, Inc.

Leonard, R. Att. (1995). *Money Trouble: Legal Strategies to Cope with Your Debts.* (third edition). New York: Nolo Press Berkeley.

Office of the Illinois Attorney General, Consumer Fraud Bureau.

Ogburn, W.P. (1996). *Fair Credit Reporting Act* (supplement). Boston: National Consumer Law Center, Inc.

Pilot, K. (1992). *Credit Approved.* Holbrook: Bob Adams, Inc.

Practicing Law Institute (1993). *Consumer Credit 1993.* New York: Practicing Law Institute.

Rumbler, B. (November 23, 1997). "Credit governs loan rate in new system." *Chicago Sun-Times,* Section C, p. 3.

Sanford, C.M. (March, 1997). "No justice." *Chicago Sun-Times,* Commentary Section, p.28.

Sheldon, J. (1994). *Fair Credit Reporting Act.* (third edition). Boston: National Consumer Law Center, Inc.

Srinivasan, K. (November 23, 1997). "College students learn hard lessons from credit cards." *Chicago Sun-Times,* Section H.

Stanley, D.T. and Girth, M. (1971). *Bankruptcy: Problem, Process, Reform.* Washington, D.C.: The Brookings Institution.

Sullivan, T. A., Warren E., and Westbrook, J. L. (1989). *As We Forgive Our Debtors: Bankruptcy and Consumer Credit in America.* New York: Oxford University Press.

TFIC. Secured Credit Card Marketing Scams. [Online] Available *www.tap.net/~hyslo/securecc.htm.* 1998.

Trans-Union. [Online] Available *www.trans union.com.* 1998.

Wagner, L. (November 21, 1997). "Credit report brings back some old headaches." *Chicago Sun-Times,* Section H, p. 7.

Index